DONNA KUIZENGA

# NARRATIVE STRATEGIES IN
## *LA PRINCESSE DE CLÈVES*

**FFM 2**

FRENCH FORUM, PUBLISHERS

**NARRATIVE STRATEGIES IN**
*LA PRINCESSE DE CLÈVES*

FRENCH FORUM MONOGRAPHS

2

*Editors*  R.C. LA CHARITÉ and V.A. LA CHARITÉ

# NARRATIVE STRATEGIES IN
## *LA PRINCESSE DE CLÈVES*

by
DONNA KUIZENGA

FRENCH FORUM, PUBLISHERS
LEXINGTON, KENTUCKY

Library of Congress Catalog Card Number 76-17258

ISBN 0-917058-01-1

*Printed in the United States of America*

# PREFACE

While *La Princesse de Clèves* has long been the subject of analysis and controversy, in recent years a number of studies have appeared reevaluating the novel from the perspectives of current criticism (1). Two scholars in particular have, in different ways, shed new light on Madame de Lafayette's style. Susan W. Tiefenbrun's work (2) on this largely neglected aspect of *La Princesse de Clèves* is done principally within the framework of Michael Riffaterre's structural and stylistic methods. The major thrust of Tiefenbrun's investigations is structural. Roger Francillon, in his *L'Oeuvre romanesque de Madame de La Fayette* (Paris: Corti, 1973), seeks to use point of view as redefined in the 1960's, notably by Wayne Booth, to gain a better understanding of the novel's workings. Both scholars are illuminating on many points, but neither focuses on what might be called Madame de Lafayette's narrative strategies in *La Princesse de Clèves*.

The present study treats narrative strategy in terms of the shaping of the reader's perspective and the functioning of irony and description. My point of departure is basically phenomenological (3), beginning with the premise that an understanding of any work of literature must be grounded in the text itself. Although it would be foolish to contend that everything in a great work is great, it is legitimate to say that every element of a text, without exception, plays an integral part in the effect produced on the reader.

If literary language is language whose potentialities are actualized by context, then an examination of *La Princesse de Clèves* requires reference not only to contemporary usage, but also to the correlations found within the text (4). The goal of this detailed examination of specific aspects of the novel is a new and clearer understanding of *La Princesse de Clèves* in terms of narrative strategy. This analysis seeks to show, in a substantive way, how the classical ideal *plaire et toucher*, is related to the novel.

I would like to offer special thanks to Professor Robert W. Hartle of Queens College and the Graduate Center, CUNY, for his guidance in the writing of the original version of this study. Professor Jules Brody, Queens College and the Graduate Center, CUNY, is also deserving of thanks for his judicious help in revising the manuscript, as are Professors Henri Peyre, Graduate Center, and Alex Szogyi, Graduate Center and Hunter College, CUNY, for their continuing interest and counsel. This project was funded in part by a grant from the Research Council of the Graduate School, University of Missouri-Columbia.

# CONTENTS

# PART I

## PERSPECTIVE: Point of View and Esthetic Distance

### Anecdote of the Jar

I placed a jar in Tennessee,
And round it was, upon a hill.
It made the slovenly wilderness
Surround that hill.

The wilderness rose up to it,
And sprawled around, no longer wild.
The jar was round upon the ground
And tall and of a port in air.

It took dominion everywhere.
The jar was gray and bare.
It did not give of bird or bush,
Like nothing else in Tennessee.

Wallace Stevens

# INTRODUCTION

When a reader first opens *La Princesse de Clèves*, he probably feels little uneasiness about the apparently uniform voice of the novel. Here is a typical passage:

Quel poison, pour Mme de Clèves, que le discours de Mme la Dauphine! Le moyen de ne se pas reconnoître pour cette personne dont on ne sçavoit point le nom et le moyen de n'estre pas pénétrée de reconnoissance et de tendresse, en apprenant, par une voye qui ne luy pouvoit estre suspecte, que ce prince, qui touchoit déjà son cœur, cachoit sa passion à tout le monde, et négligeoit pour l'amour d'elle les espérances d'une couronne. Aussi ne peut-on représenter ce qu'elle sentit, et le trouble qui s'éleva dans son âme. Si Mme la Dauphine l'eût regardée avec attention, elle eust aisément remarqué que les choses qu'elle venoit de dire ne luy estoient pas indifférentes; mais, comme elle n'avoit aucun soupçon de la vérité, elle continua de parler, sans y faire de réflexion (1).

If the reader stops to reflect, he finds himself in a maze of changes in narrative strategy. The first sentence seems to be the work of an emotionally involved storyteller. The second resembles free indirect discourse, and the third appears to be the intervention of the writer rather than the narrator (2). In the fourth sentence, the narrator, now uninvolved, picks up the train of the story (3).

Although a number of recent works on *La Princesse de Clèves* have given some attention to point of view, no full examination of narrative strategy has been made (4). If it is true that an essential part of any novelist's art is to persuade the reader to view experience in a certain way (5), the question of narrative strategy may be approached through two complementary concepts: point of view and esthetic distance.

Tzvetan Todorov considers point of view part of the verbal aspect of an utterance, and states that it can sometimes, but not always, be grasped through stylistic properties (6). He also reminds us that the structure of a novel cannot be correctly understood without an awareness of the «niveau appréciatif» or implied attitude of the narrator (7). David Daiches defines esthetic distance as «an implicit set of directions concerning the distance from the object at which the reader must stand if he is to see it for what it is» (8). Since point of view deals with angle of vision and, joined with distance, forms perspective, these two aspects of the novel prove to be complementary. Perspective is the product of Mme de Lafayette's narrative strategy. To provide a coherent study of perspective, it is necessary to retrace the reader's progress through the novel looking for techniques of implicit orientation.

*Chapter I*

# EXTERIOR VIEWS (TOME I)

The opening passages of the novel live up to the appraisal given by the author herself: «cest une parfaite imitation du monde de la court et de la maniere dont on y vit il ny a rien de romanesque et de grimpé, aussi nest ce pas un roman cest proprement des memoires et cestoit, a ce que lon ma dit, le tiltre du livre, mais on la changé» (1). The third-person narration is broken by the personifying *je*: «ce qui rendoit cette cour belle et majestueuse, estoit le nombre infiny de princes et de grands seigneurs d'un mérite extraordinaire. Ceux que je vais nommer estoient, en des manières différentes, l'ornement et l'admiration de leur siècle» (p. 8: 4-8). Reinforced by the subsequent *nos* (2), the *je* serves to minimally dramatize the narrator (Booth, p. 152; cf. Francillon, pp. 94-95).

The reader seems to be embarked on an historical journey similar to the one found in the *Vie de la Princesse d'Angleterre*. The first *persona* is the historical narrator, the memorialist. She is at a certain temporal distance from the period described (3), but her laudatory tone shows a marked sympathy for the subject (see Francillon, pp. 130, 151).

How is the reader of the seventeenth or twentieth century to react to this initial *persona*? While the historical setting as a whole may indeed, for the seventeenth-century reader at least, have implied a certain verisimilitude (4), the particular convention of pseudo-memoirs is but one of the several possible refinements of the tradition of presenting fiction in the guise of historical documents. Regardless of what seventeenth- or twentieth-century man may consider historical accuracy to be (similarity or difference), the reader knows he is dealing with fiction and accords a minimal suspension of disbelief from the outset.

The reader is enticed by the promising setting and curious about the title character. The very conventionality of the narrator's repeated hyperbole gives the impression of predictability. The narrator gives just a touch of ironic commentary here and there (5), and the reader feels initially quite sure of his ground with this decorous but not lifeless *persona*.

In conventional fashion the portraits are completed, the political situation introduced, and the reader is treated to a bit of direct discourse (p. 16: 12-19), significantly the words of Nemours, whose initial presentation has centered a particular degree of interest on him.

The much-analyzed presentation of the heroine contains the first significant modifications in point of view. For the first time, the narrator does not give simply her opinion as sufficient characterization. In the initial sentence of the presentation, «Il parut alors une beauté à la cour, qui attira les yeux de tout le monde, et l'on doit croire que c'étoit une beauté parfaite, puisqu'elle donna de l'admiration dans un lieu où l'on estoit si accoutumé à voir de belles personnes» (p. 17: 1-5), the heroine is seen just as a member of the court would have seen her (6). The impersonal construction emphasizes her entrance as an unknown quantity, whose initial presence is wholly visual. Thus, the impersonal and neutral subject *il* emphasizes the verb, while the postposed adverb underlines the antonomasia, *une beauté*.

The clause, «et l'on doit croire que c'étoit une beauté parfaite,» constitutes the first time the narrator chooses to justify an opinion, the evidence for which is given in the rest of the sentence. While all the other characters are presented as flat conventional figures who have apparently been labeled once and for all, the heroine's interiority is unexplored. Save for the novel's title, she is as yet not named. The first two antonomasiae (*beauté*, p. 17: 1 and *héritière*, p. 17: 6) are followed by references to the character in terms of her relation to others (the Vidame, her father, her mother), and then by a repetition of *héritière* (p. 18: 12). The lack of individuality in the presentation of Mlle de Chartres arouses in the reader the same curiosity felt by the courtiers (7) and, thus, momentarily binds narrator, courtier and reader in one vision. Until this point in the novel, the memorialist has described the court as an outside observer, but here the perspective shifts. Because, from this first instant the reader does not see the heroine through the same eyes as he saw the other characters, his relationship to her is special. In comparison, the presentation of Nemours, while more detailed than that of the other characters, does not depart from the mode of direct hyperbole used for the others:

> Ce prince estoit un chef-d'œuvre de la nature; ce qu'il avoit de moins admirable, c'estoit d'être l'homme du monde le mieux fait et le plus beau. Ce qui le mettoit au-dessus des autres estoit une valeur incomparable, et un agréement dans son esprit, dans son visage et dans ses actions que l'on n'a jamais veu qu'à luy seul. (p. 10: 10-16)

The very accumulation of exterior detail which can be seen in this section of the presentation differs from the paucity of external description in the presentation of the heroine, where more attention is devoted to Mme de Chartres's principles than to her daughter's attributes.

In this quotation, and again later in the presentation of Nemours, the pronoun *on* appears (8), as it does in the description of Mlle de Chartres. The pronoun functions in two different ways. In the two cases found in the presentation of Nemours, it is clear that by *on* the narrator is referring to Nemours's contemporaries. The pronoun appears in hyperboles, which by their categorical nature exclude the reader.

In contrast, in the statement, «l'on doit croire que c'étoit une beauté parfaite,» the pronoun includes the narrator's audience, the reader. Instead of excluding him, making of him a passive spectator, the narrator now invites the reader's active participation.

The narrator's initial refusal to inform in the same way, her introduction of pseudo-evidence (the verisimilitude of the preceding pages has already been accepted), and the new orientation prepare the reader for the upcoming modifications in the *récit*.

But lest the optic change too rapidly, temporarily blurring the reader's vision, the following two sentences realign the novel's world through the mediation of the memorialist: «Elle [Mlle de Chartres] estoit de la mesme maison que le Vidame de Chartres et une des plus grandes héritières de France. Son père estoit mort jeune, et l'avoit laissée sous la conduite de Mme de Chartres, sa femme, dont le bien, la vertu et le mérite estoient extraordinaires» (p. 17: 5-9). While the first sentence foreshortened the esthetic distance between the reader and Henri II's court, the initial proportions are quickly restored by the return to straightforward hyperbole.

This restoration serves also as the transitional passage following which the omniscient narrator will partially emerge from the memorialist *persona*. The presentation of the heroine is particularly rich in modifications of perspective. The generalization «La pluspart des mères s'imaginent qu'il suffit de ne parler jamais de galanterie devant les jeunes personnes pour les en éloigner» (p. 17: 15-17) is inserted into the description of Mme de Chartres's educational philosophy. While all the courtiers have been presented as conventionally exceptional, and Mlle de Chartres as unusually noteworthy for her beauty, only the mother is shown to be different in a more substantial way (9). The generalization blends the narrator's viewpoint with Mme de Chartres's, thus giving her principles added authority (10).

As the perspective shifts back to the court once again (p. 18: 12), the narrator finally names the protagonist (p. 18: 19), identifying her, although not individualizing her more clearly. This gradual progression parallels the development of the courtiers' knowledge of the newcomer.

In the presentation of Mlle de Chartres, point of view is modified in two ways. First, the insertion of Mme de Chartres's conception of *galanterie* introduces a new perspective on the court:

> Elle [Mme de Chartres] faisoit souvent à sa fille des peintures de l'Amour;
> elle luy montroit ce qu'il a d'agréable pour la persuader plus aisément sur
> ce qu'elle luy en apprenoit de dangereux; elle luy contoit le peu de sincéri-
> té des hommes, leurs tromperies et leur infidélité, les malheurs domesti-
> ques où plongent les engagemens; et elle luy faisoit voir, d'un autre côté,
> quelle tranquillité suivoit la vie d'une honneste femme, et combien la vertu
> donnoit d'éclat et d'élévation à une personne qui avoit de la beauté et de
> la naissance; mais elle luy faisoit voir aussi combien il estoit difficile de con-
> server cette vertu, que par une extrême défiance de soy-mesme et par un
> grand soin de s'attacher à ce qui seul peut faire le bonheur d'une femme,
> qui est d'aimer son mary et d'en estre aimée. (pp. 17: 18-18: 11)

While initially the memorialist's ironic comments about the no-
bles added an attractive *malveillance* to the tone, the reader's vision of the court is now modified by a serious critique of *la galanterie*.

Secondly, however, in order to balance this condemnation of
court *liaisons*, the narrator separates herself from Mme de Chartres's point of view and, in the physical description of the Princess (p. 18: 18-24), returns to conventional exterior hyperbole,
as with the other characters. Were the narrator merely to aban-
don her previous admiring attitude towards the court in favor of
Mme de Chartres's viewpoint, one element of the novel's central
conflict would be eliminated. If social life were presented as
worthless from the outset, the force of the *dénouement* would
be somewhat diminished (Woshinsky, p. 66). Further, such a
radical alteration in the narrator's stance would destroy any uni-
ty of the perspective.

The first modification of esthetic distance and point of view
was found in the presentation of Mlle de Chartres. Through a
generalization, the narrator's viewpoint blends with that of
Mme de Chartres. In the scene at the jewel merchant's, generalization occurs again. Mlle de Chartres is seen through M. de Clèves's eyes. The narrator, however, intervenes with a generalization: «Il [the Prince] s'apperceut que ses regards l'embarrassoient
[Mlle de Chartres], contre l'ordinaire des jeunes personnes qui
voyent toujours avec plaisir l'effet de leur beauté» (p. 19: 15-
17). The reflexion is a rational explanation of Mlle de Chartres's

difference as perceived by the Prince. In this way the heroine's modesty is foregrounded (11).

A number of fairly clear examples of narrator intervention are to be found in Part I. Once the initial description of the court has been completed, the techniques of attenuation (e.g. *il semblait, il lui paraissait*) become more frequent. In the opening passages, judgmental description is the primary narrative mode. With the presentation of the heroine, the narrator becomes more reticent, and consequently her direct commentary becomes more significant.

In addition to the two generalizations just discussed, the narrator espouses the evaluation of the Princess' beauty previously presented as the courtiers' reaction: «Lorsqu'elle arriva, le Vidame alla au-devant d'elle; il fut surpris de la grande beauté de Mlle de Chartres, et il en fut surpris avec raison» (p. 18: 18-20). Within the conventions of the novel, the heroine's uniqueness, on the exterior level, has acquired the status of fact.

The author underlines her uniqueness on the moral plane by the generalization in the scene at the jeweler's. Thus, when the narrator states, «Mlle de Chartres avoit le cœur très noble et très bien fait» (p. 30: 22-23), the comment indicates the perspective in which the heroine's apparently favorable disposition toward M. de Clèves is to be seen. The narrator defends the heroine against any accusation of bad faith. This perspective is elaborated in the ensuing description of the Prince's haste to believe what he wishes (p. 30: 24-29).

In describing the heroine's relationship to the Chevalier de Guise, the narrator intervenes twice more to solidify further the favorable evaluation of Mlle de Chartres's character. Her pity for Guise is justified: «il [Guise] avoit tant de mérite et tant d'agréement qu'il estoit difficile de le rendre malheureux sans en avoir quelque pitié» (p. 32: 29-31). Both Mme de Chartres and the narrator admire the Princess' sincerity: «Mme de Chartres admiroit la sincérité de sa fille, et elle l'admiroit avec raison, car jamais personne n'en a eu une si grande et si naturelle» (p. 33: 1-3). Here, as in the description of Mme de Chartres's education of her daughter, the narrator's orientation parallels that of the mother.

The expression *il estoit difficile* constitutes a less forceful intervention than does *avec raison*. Just as the proportion of direct intervention decreases as the initial attitudes are established, so the directness of the statements themselves is attenuated. The heroine's feelings for men other than her husband are justified by interventions using *il estoit difficile* (12). The locution is initially used in a purely factual sense (the Queen «avoit une si profonde dissimulation qu'*il estoit difficile* de juger de ses sentimens,» p. 6: 16-17), and then in the less significant justification in reference to Guise (p. 32: 29-31). As a result, the comments on the *coup de foudre* are less obtrusive. The mutual reaction of the Duke and heroine at the ball contains the locution twice: «Ce prince estoit fait d'une sorte qu'*il estoit difficile* de n'estre pas surprise de le voir quand on ne l'avoit jamais vu, surtout ce soir-là, où le soin qu'il avoit pris de se parer augmentoit encore l'air brillant qui estoit dans sa personne; mais *il estoit difficile* aussi de voir Mme de Clèves pour la première fois sans avoir un grand étonnement» (pp. 35: 33-36: 5).

Only once more in Part I does the narrator intervene directly, to provide yet more justification for the heroine's love of Nemours. Again the expression *il estoit difficile* appears, this time after a more expanded commentary (p. 38: 1-9). Unless a reasonable basis is laid for the *coup de foudre* the Princess' struggle will lose its dramatic power. She cannot, like Titania, fall in love with Bottom. Not only must the passion be irresistible, its object must appear worthy in the reader's eyes. The narrator's direct intervention gives these justifications the force of fact.

In these two passages dealing with Nemours and Mme de Clèves (pp. 35: 33-36: 5; 38: 1-8), almost all of the attention is devoted to a description of Nemours. This sort of unequal distribution has the effect of showing the situation essentially from the heroine's perspective. For example, while the ball scene is narrated from Mme de Clèves's point of view, it is not a question of an inside view, since the heroine's feelings are still undefined (Woshinsky, p. 109). Her love for Nemours is justified in some detail, while the Duke's attraction to Mme de Clèves merely depends on the foregoing descriptions of her. The reader's interest is centered on the birth of passion in the heroine, while it is made to seem only natural that Nemours should be attracted to her.

In several passages, the narrator intervenes in such a way as to appear almost indistinguishable from a certain character. The clearest example is provided by the reflexions on the court. The passage opens with the statement, «Mme de Chartres, qui avoit eu tant d'application pour inspirer la vertu à sa fille, ne discontinua pas de prendre les mesmes soins dans un lieu où ils estoient si nécessaires et où il y avoit tant d'exemples si dangereux» (p. 23: 14-18). The reader is given no indication whether the judgments are those of Mme de Chartres or of the narrator. The subsequent reflexions on the court, fused with additional scene-setting material, cannot as such be considered a phase of Mme de Chartres's thought. Through the indetermination of the above sentence, however, the two points of view are merged, and the additional authority of such statements gives even more weight to Mme de Chartres's attitudes. In a subsequent passage, as Rousset points out (p. 41), Mme de Chartres, through her perspicacity, appears to take over the narrator's function. When the daughter makes no mention of Nemours's feelings for her, «Mme de Chartres ne le voyoit que trop, aussi bien que le penchant que sa fille avoit pour lui» (pp. 46: 35-47: 1). Here again the shared perspective adds authority to Mme de Chartres's views (cf. Woshinsky, p. 105; Francillon, p. 97).

This valuation sets in motion one of the novel's ironic structures. Initially, the reader is led to accept Mme de Chartres's moral position as valid, in much the same way that her daughter does. On the one hand, this is, like the focusing of much of the direct discourse, a means by which the reader shares the heroine's perception of reality. On the other hand, the reader knows, always a little before Mme de Chartres, the degree of Mme de Clèves's attachment to Nemours. The initial presentation of Nemours prepares this. The narrator's description of the couple's first meeting (pp. 35: 30-36: 5) and the placement of the Chevalier de Guise's surmise (p. 37: 3-14) succeed, without ever using direct statement, in giving the reader a clear idea of the situation. Mme de Chartres's perception, placed after the narrator's comments, the court's reaction to the couple, the introductions, and the passage concerning Guise, arrives for the reader with the same «retard fatal» of which Rousset (p. 30) speaks in relation to Mme de Clèves's reflexions.

Consequently, the reader has some fair notion of the ineffectiveness of the mother's efforts, from the ball scene on. Not only does this put Mme de Chartres in an ironic light, it also casts retroactive irony on the older woman's judgment that she gave her daughter «un mary qu'elle . . . pûst aimer» (p. 31: 7-8) (13). The approbation with which Mme de Chartres is treated shows her to the reader in the light in which her daughter sees both the woman and her ideals. Unless Mme de Chartres's values are made to seem worthwhile to the reader, the heroine's struggle might appear to be motivated only by a fear of passion and its attendant jealousy, with moral considerations serving only as a mask the heroine puts on her fears. The irony is also important in the shape of the whole novel, which leads the reader to question, not Mme de Clèves's virtue, but any possibility of finding fulfillment in life (14).

The narrator's interventions represent one kind of directions orienting the reader's perspective. This orientation may be more or less explicit, as shown by the contrast between *il estoit difficile* and *avec raison*. The interventions modify the flow of the narrative by altering the mode of the relationship between reader and narrator. Direct discourse contrasts with the narrative by its form, and this contrast results in an alteration of the relationship between reader and narrative, in the sense that the foregrounding effect of direct discourse commands an increased degree of attention. The use of direct discourse also plays a role in the orientation of the reader. Unlike the narrator's interventions, the orientation afforded by direct discourse is wholly implicit.

In the first instance of direct discourse—Nemours's reply to the King on the subject of a possible match with Elizabeth (p. 16: 12-19)—the change in the mode of the narrative focuses increased attention on Nemours, specifically on his modesty (seen in his words themselves), and in a larger sense, on his desirability, evidenced by the English Queen's interest.

Mme de Lafayette's use of direct discourse can do much more than merely focus attention on a fact of the plot (cf. Francillon, pp. 122-23, 163). The second instance of direct speech seems at first an almost illogical choice. In the scene at Madame's in which the Prince is first introduced to Mlle de Chartres, Madame's words to M. de Clèves are in direct form: «Venez . . . voyez si je ne vous tiens pas ma parole et si, en vous montrant Mlle de Chartres, je ne vous fais pas voir cette beauté que vous cherchiez; remerciez-moy au moins de luy avoir appris l'admiration que vous aviez déjà pour elle» (p. 21: 14-18). The Prince's compliments, however, are presented in indirect discourse: «il la [Mlle de Chartres] supplia de se souvenir qu'il avoit esté le premier à l'admirer et que, sans la connoître, il avoit eu pour elle tous les sentiments de respect et d'estime qui luy estoient deûs» (p. 21: 22-25). The reader has been told that the various praises she has heard so far have had little apparent effect on Mlle de Chartres: «Elle les recevoit avec une modestie si noble qu'il ne sembloit pas qu'elle les entendist, ou du moins, qu'elle en fust touchée» (p. 21: 8-10). This reinforces the emphasis which Mme de Lafayette has put on the heroine's modesty in the scene at the jewel merchant's. Keeping this in mind, one can see that the vague description of Mlle de Chartres's reception at court is an analogue of the heroine's own perception of these events. What strikes Mlle de Chartres most forcefully must be the Prince's appearance, since, at that moment, the man being described by Madame coincides with the heroine's recognition of him as the man seen at the jeweler's. Madame's rather enthusiastic remark cannot but be the focal point of Mlle de Chartres's attention. In an analogous manner, the direct discourse breaks in on the *récit* and strikes the reader. As for the Prince's compliments, once the initial shock of recognition has passed, M. de Clèves in his individuality does not move the Princess, a fact indicated by the indirect discourse. M. de Clèves is thus kept at a distance from the reader, who sees him in harmony with the heroine (on the treatment of the Prince, see Part I, Chapter IV). Without yet having recourse to interiority, Mme de Lafayette makes the reader share Mlle de Chartres's perspective.

This is the first of a series of instances in which direct discourse is structured according to the heroine's optic. The most striking statements from the Princess' point of view make up the main body of direct discourse. Such passages account for one of the principal functions of direct discourse in the novel.

There are ten more instances of direct discourse in the first part of the novel. In keeping with the gradual progress from exterior to interior, they not only break up the uniformity of the narrative, but gradually move the reader closer to the principal characters. These passages are unified by the Princess' presence. While the reader does not know her very well yet, he is slowly prepared to see much of the story from her viewpoint, though at first with no supplementary information about her interiority. He follows her steps through the mediation of the narrator (15).

The presentation of the stories of Marie de Lorraine and Diane in direct discourse gives the reader the impression that he is listening to these tales of love and intrigue with the heroine. The same situation obtains at the beginning of Part II, where, within a frame of conversation as in Mme de Chartres's *récit*, the reader hears the story of Sancerre (pp. 58: 1-70: 15).

In an analogous manner, on the evening when Mme de Clèves and the Reine Dauphine are choosing jewels for Saint-André's ball, the portions of the scene in direct discourse (the discussion of Nemours's opinions on one's mistress attending a ball, pp. 48: 4-49: 2; 49: 13-29) are precisely those to which the heroine would listen with the most attention. By limiting the use of dialogue to the essential elements, the author not only achieves streamlined plot structure, but adds formal intensity to the material most striking to the Princess. In this way, the reader, almost without realizing it, begins to share the heroine's perspective. This fact is underlined by the narrator's intervention (16). The specification of what the reader has already half-surmised provides an ironic perspective, retroactively on the first part of the dialogue, and on the subsequent passages as well. The narrator also substantiates her pretensions to objectivity, for, in the complex narrative structure, she must appear not only personalized but reliable. Her credibility, manifested in her clear-sighted omniscience, a power not always used (Niderst, pp. 76-78), is essential to the novel's irony, for through it the reader is always kept one step ahead of the characters, giving rise to a double vision.

This vision is tripled when the heroine engages in introspection. Having seen her actions, knowing all the while that they betray her, the reader sees her make the same belated discovery, and resolve to remedy the situation. The resolve becomes ever more poignant (and/or hypocritical) as the novel progresses and one sees the repeated failure of these resolves (Rousset, p. 22; Kaps, p. 63).

As in the scene at the Reine Dauphine's, one hears Mme de Chartres's parting injunctions in direct discourse, the form again miming the acuity with which these words touch the Princess (pp. 55: 33-56: 33). The same foregrounding technique is also evident in the discussion of Mme de Clèves's feigned illness (p. 51: 5-11, 20-27), the comments on Nemours's changed behavior (pp. 53: 25-54: 24), and in the transition from indirect to direct discourse when Mme de Chartres suggests to her daughter that Nemours is in love with the Reine Dauphine: «Elle [Mme de Chartres] se mit un jour à parler de lui [Nemours] ; elle lui [the Princess] en dit du bien et y mesla beaucoup de louanges empoisonnées sur la sagesse qu'il avoit d'estre incapable de devenir amoureux et sur ce qu'il ne se faisoit qu'un plaisir et non pas un attachement sérieux du commerce des femmes. Ce n'est pas, ajouta-t-elle, que l'on ne l'ait soupçonné d'avoir une grande passion pour la Reine Dauphine . . . » (p. 52: 16-23).

«La parole,» according to Fabre, «est ici le contraire d'un repos ou d'une évasion. L'auteur ne la donne à ses personnages qu'à des fins impitoyables. Pas un mot qui ne porte et qui ne blesse dans les propos qui semblent les plus futiles» (17). This analysis underlines the confluence of stylistic foregrounding and the characters' particular perspectives.

Unlike the passages discussed above, the remaining instances of direct discourse in Part I are not shaped according to the heroine's optic. Although they command special attention by virtue of their formal contrast with the third-person narrative, these passages serve primarily what might be called a plot-structuring function. Conversations between Mme de Chartres and her daughter (pp. 38: 19-40: 2), and later between the Prince and his wife (pp. 58: 1-59: 13), provide the transitions from the narrative to the tales of Diane de Poitiers and of Sancerre, respectively. Two other passages, M. de Clèves's reproaches to his fiancée over her lack of passion (pp. 31: 20-32: 12) and the conversation between Mme de Clèves, Nemours and the Reine Dauphine at the ball (p. 36: 18-32), highlight by their form important elements of the central conflict.

Using the second of these passages as an example, one can see how they present certain information to the reader:

> Pour moy, madame, dit M. de Nemours, je n'ay pas d'incertitude; mais comme Mme de Clèves n'a pas les mesmes raisons pour deviner qui je suis que celles que j'ay pour la reconnoître, je voudrois bien que Votre Majesté eust la bonté de lui apprendre mon nom.
>
> Je crois, dit Mme la Dauphine, qu'elle le sçait aussi bien que vous sçavez le sien.
>
> Je vous assure, Madame, reprit Mme de Clèves, qui paroissoit un peu embarassée, que je ne devine pas si bien que vous pensez.
>
> Vous devinez fort bien, répondit Mme la Dauphine; et il y a mesme quelque chose d'obligeant pour M. de Nemours à ne vouloir pas avouer que vous le connoissez sans l'avoir jamais veu. (p. 36: 18-32)

This dialogue resembles drama in the sense that the reader becomes a spectator, watching the various characters act. Unlike those passages in which the author shapes direct discourse according to the heroine's optic, these passages give the reader the impression that he observes the scenes from an exterior, neutral point. Consequently, the expression *balanced views* can be used to describe such scenes. If the story were presented solely from the heroine's point of view, the reader would find himself in a position of complicity with her. However, this is not the case in *La Princesse de Clèves*. The balanced scenes of direct discourse, by giving the reader the impression that he stands outside and observes, provide him with other, albeit fictive, points of reference for the orientation of his view of the heroine. In concert with the wider scope of information which the reader generally has, these balanced scenes allow the reader a certain distance from the heroine, creating irony. Later, as the characters become more conscious of their own motivations, and consequently become more active, this sort of dialogue becomes a more dominant mode of presentation (see Part I, Chapter III).

In sum, two basic uses of direct discourse in *La Princesse de Clèves* are exemplified in the first part of the novel. Although the proportions change, the fundamental purposes do not (18). The striking thing, however, is the fact that the essential foregrounding effect, foreshortening the distance between reader and *récit*, is not always connected with a single perspective. The reader may become a spectator in the balanced scenes, share the heroine's point of view in other passages, and later, will participate more intensely in interior monologues and soliloquies in the direct form (19).

This reading of Part I may seem to have digressed far from its original topics: point of view and esthetic distance. Broad, traditional classifications of narrative vision (20) do not provide much insight into the novel. The term *perspective* was chosen in order to widen the scope of this inquiry. The way the reader perceives the novel is determined by a variety of techniques, some of which have been discussed above. The general result is a shared perspective for reader and heroine. The narrator serves as an intermediary between the two, especially in those cases where Mme de Clèves is seen mostly from the outside. Only once she has met Nemours does the heroine appear endowed with interiority, but in Part I her thoughts are always rephrased by the narrator (21). Because she is omniscient, the narrator serves not only as intermediary between character and reader, but also provides that supplementary information which makes the reader's perspective wider than the heroine's. Shared perspective is therefore complemented by an ironic vision which will become more explicit as the novel progresses. If irony is indeed looking in two ways with one eye (22), it is an advantage which the reader almost always has in *La Princesse de Clèves*. This irony intensifies in Part II, as interior views become a more prevalent mode of presentation (23).

Exterior views of the heroine predominate in the first part of the novel, and both ironic vision and shared perspective arise from this same source. On the one hand, because of the absence of interiority, distance is maintained, giving rise to irony. On the other, the manipulation of many of the passages in direct discourse results in a shared perspective. In addition, the narrator's interventions create empathy with Mme de Clèves. This empathy also implies shared perspective.

*Chapter II*

## INTERIOR VIEWS (TOME II)

One of the major elements of the reader's ironic vision in *La Princesse de Clèves* is the ability to perceive the heroine's interiority without sharing that solipsism inherent in each man's view of himself. A principal theme of this novel, as in the fictional works of André Malraux, is the inability of one man to pierce another's interiority. One advantage of literature over life is that, as a reader, one may be permitted to see into the characters.

The second section of the novel presents several examples of the technique used to deal with interiority. One of the most striking is the description of Mme de Clèves's reaction to the Reine Dauphine's tale of Nemours's changed behavior (1):

1 Quel poison pour Mme de Clèves, que le discours de Mme la Dauphine! / 2a Le moyen de ne se pas reconnoître pour cette personne dont on ne sçavoit point le nom, / 2b et le moyen de n'estre pas pénétrée de reconnoissance et de tendresse, / 2c en apprenant par une voye qui ne luy pouvoit estre suspecte, / 2d que ce Prince qui touchoit déjà son cœur, / 2e cachoit sa passion à tout le monde, et négligeoit pour l'amour d'elle les espérances d'une Couronne; / 3 aussi ne peut-on représenter ce qu'elle sentit, et le trouble qui s'éleva dans son âme. / 4 Si Mme la Dauphine l'eût regardée

avec attention, elle eust aisément remarqué que les choses qu'elle venoit de
dire ne luy estoient pas indifférentes; mais comme elle n'avoit aucun soupçon de la vérité, elle continua de parler, sans y faire de réflexion. (p. 73:6-
20; P1678, II, 59-61)

The moment is important, for the Princess is disabused of any
illusion that her passion for Nemours has ceased. The passage
cited forms a unit, constituting the main portion of the narration interrupting the direct discourse.

Unless an author resorts to disruptions of syntax and various
semantic dislocations, such as metaphor and image, in order to
translate psychological states into what the twentieth century
has come to consider stream-of-consciousness (2), a character's
complex state at a point of violent emotion, felt as overwhelm-
ing, renders the narrator's intervention necessary. Mme de Lafayette chooses neither to present psychological raw material nor
to use the narrator as the «cool» translator of this material. It is
here, at a psychologically significant and emotionally charged
moment, that Mme de Lafayette uses her narrator's flexibility
to best advantage.

In unit 1, the narrator herself cries out, as the Princess cannot,
interrupting the Dauphine. The exclamation has an immediate
impact on the reader for several reasons. To begin with, it breaks
in upon the Dauphine's story and constitutes a sharp and unpre-
pared change in perspective. Secondly, as a whole it is surpris-
ingly judgmental; the reader is not accustomed to having the
narrator assert herself so forcefully. Not only does the narrator
intrude with a judgment; she frames it in the form of an emotional outburst which is most unlike her customary controlled
tone. Finally, the word *poison* (3), which is used here for the
only time in the novel, is the most strongly stressed word in the
sentence. It is all the more forceful since it is the only word in
unit 1 with possible affective content. The effect of *quel poison*
on the reader is the same shock that the character feels at the
realization that she is still as entangled as before.

While this unit is highly asymmetrical in stress and affective
content, its two clauses show a great degree of structural sym-
metry. This is consonant with the double function of the narrator, who both judges, and is affected by, the Princess' plight. It

is, of course, through this double game that the narrator succeeds both in telling the reader what she thinks and in obtaining
his emotional complicity, which brings with it intellectual agreement.

After its initial stress, the rest of unit 1 serves as a transition
between the pure narration of 1 and the new technique of presentation in unit 2. This method of presenting interiority is here
termed *secondary mimesis*. If one considers the now customary
techniques of stream-of-consciousness mentioned above to function as the highest degree to which language is capable of translating pre-speech psychological states, these techniques might be
called *primary mimesis*. What Mme de Lafayette often does,
however, is to take up a position half inside and half outside the
character's psyche (4). It is to this technique, which lies between narration and representation, that the expression *secondary mimesis* applies.

The complex structure of unit 2 must be seen in two ways.
On the one hand, the ability to express the Princess' turmoil in
a grammatically sophisticated manner is the privilege of observer over actor. On the other, the irregular flow of the unit (especially 2c and 2d) mimes the character's great agitation. By
choosing the rhetorical question form, Mme de Lafayette obtains two results. The rhetorical question sustains the emotional
tenor established by the form. In addition, a rhetorical question,
while emphatic, is not quite as forceful as an exclamation,
which admits, albeit only formally, some doubt. The effect of 2
as a whole is to sollicit both the reader's sympathy (in the etymological sense) and his understanding.

2a and 2b begin with the interrogative *le moyen*, followed in
each case by a negative. The stress accents fall on *moyen*, which
by its repetition underlines the insistence and conviction with
which the question as a whole is asked. The additional repetition of the negations, giving a and b largely parallel structure,
completes the emphatic device. By framing her questions in the
negative, the narrator, without appearing to do so, forces the
reader to agree to the naturalness of the Princess' reactions.
The narrator asks *how* Mme de Clèves could *not* have reacted as
she did (5). The unstated implication of such a question is, of

course, exclusionary: there was no alternative. Consequently, the Princess' reaction is seen as natural, indeed inevitable. The reader, in turn, by nature of his situation (he cannot, like the author, control the character), is incapable of supplying *le moyen* and forced to accede.

One of the most interesting aspects of the initial portions of 2 is the ambiguity of the subject. The *se* in 2a designates Mme de Clèves. Grammatically, however, 2a and 2b appear to begin a question couched in purely impersonal terms. The aphoristic tone, and the generality of sense thus obtained, make it appear for a moment that the reader is dealing with a truism in which *se* could be anyone or everyone. In this way, Mme de Clèves's reaction is also justified, since it is presented almost as though it were a general law of humanity, and not an individual case.

Whereas in 2a the stress accent falls on *le moyen*, while the rest of the clause receives fairly uniform stress, providing another hiatus before the repetition of the interrogation, in 2b while *le moyen* is stressed by virtue of its initial position and of its repetition both *reconnoissance* and *tendresse* receive at least equal stress. Both substantives are most significant for the description of the heroine's emotions, and for the reader's appraisal of her new fall into passion. Here, however, *passion* is applied (in 2e) not to Mme de Clèves, but to Nemours. The more elliptical *touchoit . . . son cœur* is in keeping with the Princess' state of awareness (6). The heroine is filled with one entirely laudable emotion, *reconnoissance*, and a gentle, and usually connotatively virtuous one, *tendresse* (7). If, then, Mme de Clèves loves someone she should not, it cannot be said that the emotion which she feels is in itself in any way unworthy. The reader does not see a woman in the throes of passion, but one filled with gratitude and tenderness for a man who has, as will be reiterated in 2e, provided her, in her absence, with exceptional proofs of his disinterested love. In the psychological evolution of the novel, the progress from interest through gratitude and tenderness is the route which, as in *La Carte de Tendre*, Mme de Clèves must travel in order to come to a full consciousness of her situation.

While unit 1 is symmetrical in clause length, unit 2 is com-

posed of irregular parts: they are neither symmetrical, nor do
they combine to form a *cadence majeure* (8). The rhythmic patterns are mimetic. The initial shock of feeling (*quel poison*) is
followed by a brief hesitation (the rest of 1). A second, less intense and more prolonged rush of thought and feeling is por-
trayed in 2. As in any situation which produces a sudden emotional shock, the initial blow is followed by a disorganized rush
of reactions, both emotional and intellectual, before the impact
of the trigger event lessens sufficiently to allow some control.
Clauses 2a and 2b, with the slowing at the end of b, illustrate
rhythmically a second rush of feeling, which gradually slows to
an irregular series of clauses, 2c and d, which imitate in rhythm
that emotional state in which the various aspects of the disturb-
ing situation are perceived analogically and strung together until
some, at least provisional, conclusion can be reached. This process provides transition from the predominantly emotional to
the predominantly intellectual reaction to the trigger event. In
2, of course, Mme de Lafayette has organized the psychological
raw material. Through rhythm, she succeeds in making the reader share in Mme de Clèves's agitation.

2c is most fundamental to the creation of this impression.
The extremely short *en apprenant* disrupts the flow of the sentence. The following phrase, *par une voye qui ne luy pouvoit estre suspecte*, appears to announce a new *cadence majeure*, although it is somewhat long in contrast to *en apprenant* to form
a pattern of gradually increasing length. 2c is thus in itself lacking in relative equilibrium and it sets up a false rhythmic expectation. In addition, the *luy* serves as a transition between the
impersonal structure of 2a and b, and the personal presence giv-
en the character by *elle* (2e). The brief *que ce Prince* of 2d again
breaks the flow, and consequently brings a rhythmic relief
which is analogous to the place Nemours occupies in the mind
of Mme de Clèves. *Prince* receives the strongest stress accent in
2d.

If 2c sets up the false expectation of a *cadence majeure*, whose
absence disturbs the reader's sense of rhythm (9), and, therefore,
causes him to feel an analogue of the character's disturbance,
clause 2d does in fact begin a *cadence majeure* which will run

through 2e to the end of the unit. The narrator gradually regains control and places herself farther from the character. This gradual «damping» of the narrative's emotional tone is crucial to the effects produced by the passage as a whole. In both rhythm and content, 2d and e and 3 move toward ever increasing rational control, maintaining a degree of irony.

In 2e the anticipated justification of Mme de Clèves's reaction, held in suspense by the second elements of both 2c and 2d, is finally presented. These two delays, of course, increase the tension implicit during the elaboration of any interrogation which one is expected to answer, as the rhetorical question is here directed at the reader. In the first part of 2e, a stress accent falls on passion, the essential concept. Mme de Clèves's feelings are justified, at least in part, by the veracity and force of Nemours's love. The mystery which for everyone else clouds Nemours's behavior, no longer eludes the Princess, who has now received an account of it which she cannot doubt, thus ironically robbing her of the very suspicions which might have assured her safety. She and Nemours form a unit separate from the rest of the world. In 2a, Mme de Clèves is differentiated from the general on, who do not know the identity of Nemours's beloved. In 2e, this differentiation is more forcefully underlined by the hyperbolic *à tout le monde*.

The latter portion of 2e presents the justification for Mme de Clèves's feelings of gratitude, just as Nemours's secrecy has justified her tenderness. The final section (2e) can be divided into two main parts (*pour l'amour d'elle / les espérances*), with stress accents falling on *elle* and *espérances*. Here, *elle* is the crucial element, since in the Princess' mind, the most important fact, finally stated directly, is that Nemours acts out of affection for *her*. The final element of the question, *les espérances d'une Couronne*, gives proof of the greatness of Nemours's love and partially justifies Mme de Clèves's passion. The rhetorical question is terminated by the more exterior, and grander justification. Had the order of 2e been reversed, this effect would have been lost.

In unit 3, the form of the narrator's statement passes from exclamation through rhetorical question, to a perorational declarative. But while oration often begins intellectually and ends emotionally, Mme de Lafayette here follows a contrary route, and, as is more suitable to her purposes, ends on an abstract, detached note. The initial *aussi* announces the summarizing function of what is to follow. The reader, whose participation has already been required by 2, is now again involved by the use of *on*. The hyperbolic statement in 3 adds a new and undefined perspective to the portrait of Mme de Clèves's reaction. The intensity of the heroine's feelings is stressed as the reader is told that they cannot be adequately communicated. The statement made in 3 is, of course, specious, since the passage itself succeeds in representing most precisely what Mme de Clèves felt. The reader, perceiving the difference between what the narrator says and what she has just done, steps back from her. The resulting ironic distance signals the beginning of the transition from interiority back to exteriority.

If both *ce qu'elle sentit* and *le trouble* share a relative degree of abstraction, they are not equivalent expressions. At first appearance they seem to be so because syntactically parallel, but, while *ce qu'elle sentit* is indeed the epitome of colorlessness and objectivity, reinforcing the controlled tone already established by *aussi* and *on, le trouble* has connotative as well as denotative value. Because the substantive has more than one meaning, its denotation, here agitation, is contaminated by the connotation that this state is less than pleasant. Unit 2 showed the Princess under the influence of basically agreeable emotions. The paradox of the situation is that Mme de Clèves does not wish to feel these things. At this precise moment, however, the character is not yet far enough from the initial flood of feeling to condemn herself for it. The author, therefore, provides the judgmental material by the use of the word *poison*, by the presence of a rhetorical question implying that the Princess' state requires some kind of justification, and by choosing *trouble* as the final description of her state. Mme de Lafayette, naturally, does no more than imply that the Princess' immediate sentiments, and her subsequent judgments of them, are to be at odds, but these implications, strengthened by what is already known of the heroine's attitude towards her passion, are sufficient to add an ironic perspective to the description. It is impossible for the character to be aware of this irony in these first moments of her reaction, in any other way than perhaps a vague tinge of regret which mixes with the tenderness and gratitude. The irony is, therefore, dramatic since the reader does not forget, as Mme de Clèves momentarily does, that she has but recently imagined her feelings for Nemours to be no more (see p. 70: 12-22). There is also an element of complicity in this irony since, by the techniques mentioned above, Mme de Lafayette reminds the reader that the situation must be seen from more than one point of view.

Unit 4 serves as a transition, preparing for the Dauphine's next remarks, which will alter the Princess' psychological state. The intensity of the first rush of feeling is illustrated by Mme de Clèves's inability to dissimulate completely. As the narrator passes from interior to exterior, she underlines the convention of omniscience in unit 4, thus giving the characters' behavior an added air of reality, which combines with the foregrounding effect of direct discourse.

On the whole, the success of this passage is based on the use of multiple and constantly shifting perspectives. In addition to the author's ironic perspective, the reader has the narrator's privilege of sympathizing with the character, and justifying her reaction. The passage itself, especially in unit 2, mimes the Princess' feelings, while rephrasing them for the reader, and thus creates a third perspective, that of Mme de Clèves. The reader sees more than does the character, but he looks in those directions towards which Mme de Lafayette has turned him, participating in Mme de Clèves's reality.

In Part II there are two more examples of the technique of secondary mimesis applied to the heroine's psychological states. After Nemours steals the portrait, the Prince jokingly remarks that his wife must have given it to a lover. This comment sets off a series of guilty reactions in Mme de Clèves. The passage itself (pp. 88: 17-89: 7) moves from initial general statements to that interiority provided by secondary mimesis, and then to a gradual distancing sequence. The following lines comprise the interiorizing sequence:

1 Ces paroles, quoy que dites en riant, firent une vive impression dans l'esprit de Mme de Clèves: / 2 Elles lui donnèrent des remords; / 3 elle fit réflexion à la violence de l'inclination qui l'entraînoit vers M. de Nemours; / 4 elle trouva qu'elle n'estoit plus maîtresse de ses paroles et de son visage; / 5 elle pensa que Lignerolles estoit revenu; / 6 qu'elle ne craignoit plus l'affaire d'Angleterre; / 7 qu'elle n'avoit plus de soupçons sur Mme la Dauphine; / 8 qu'enfin il n'y avoit plus rien qui la pust deffendre, / 9 et qu'il n'y avoit de seureté pour elle qu'en s'éloignant. (p. 88: 17-26; P1678, II, 129-30)

In unit 1 the narrator announces the theme. Unit 2 defines it, but the voice is still that of an objective and exterior narrator who sees things as they are and can call them by their names. The brevity of unit 2 (in contrast to 1) translates some of the sharpness with which the Prince's comments strike his wife, but the affective capacity of 2 is minimal.

Unit 3 constitutes the first step toward interiority. The narrator, in the middle distance between interior and exterior, can now comment obliquely on the material presented. This technique orients the reader but, unlike the cases of obvious intervention, does so in a more subversive way. On the one hand, unit 3 does not appear to differ from unit 2. They both seem to be intellectual resumés by the narrator of the character's state of mind. However, the expression *elle fit réflexion* serves to distinguish between narrator and character. While in unit 2 the Princess is an object of analysis, in unit 3 she returns to her position as actress in her own drama. This initial expression in unit 3 prepares the reader for the more direct presentation of the character's thoughts. Nonetheless, the particular structure chosen, *faire réflexion à quelque chose*, presupposes that the general theme of the reflexions, rather than the thoughts themselves, will be stated. Therefore, although the Princess regains an active position in unit 3, the narrator continues to intervene in the form of an analytical intellect, providing a summary of the character's thoughts. The use of *la violence de l'inclination* rather than *l'inclination violente* gives evidence of the narrator's control. The substantivation of that aspect of the heroine's love essential to her present thoughts implies the intervention of an analytical, unaffected mind.

Similarly, the verb *entraîner* summarizes an analysis of the situation. It not only reinforces the notion of violence, but conveys the Princess' resistance to her passion and her inability to prevent herself from being governed by it. The combination of the anteposition of *la violence* and the use of *entraîner* serves to crystallize the image of passion presented here. The reader comprehends, intellectually, that it is felt by the character as a violation which she is incapable of preventing.

Unit 4 is the first statement proceeding, apparently without intervention, from the Princess' mind. The gradual movement from general to specific is maintained unbroken. First the narrator announces the character's state (units 1 and 2), then one moves gradually toward the particulars (units 3 through 7) before a new distancing sequence is begun (units 8 and 9). The second and third steps of this procedure mime the usual psychological process. The first step represents the imposition of an additional layer of rationality and control so that each section of interiority (the secondary mimesis which functions as a mask for irrationality) is framed, and thus kept within certain boundaries (10). It is not that the irrational has been banished from the novel, but that it is stylized so as to appear rational (11).

Part of the conclusion to be drawn in units 8 and 9 is presented in 4. The heroine's sense of helplessness, voiced by the narrator in 3, is now repeated by the Princess through the use of *ne plus etre maîtresse* (see Kaps, pp. 7-8; Tiefenbrun, «The Art,» pp. 49-50). Units 5 through 7 constitute the specific instances on which the heroine will base her judgments, and their common subordination, as well as their approximately uniform length, help to indicate the Princess' agitation. This rhythm is broken by *enfin* in 8, and it sets, together with the coordinating *et* at the beginning of 9, the last two units apart. The intensified negative *plus rien* renders the conclusion more categorical and adds force to the statement of the only solution, since the *ne . . . que* continues the series of negations.

Between 8 and 9 the heroine passes from analysis to a virtual, or hypothetical, decision which is then contradicted by the ensuing passage, giving the appearance of a decision followed by a peripety. Here is the subsequent passage:

1 Mais, comme elle n'estoit pas maîtresse de s'éloigner, / 2 elle se trouvoit dans une grande extrémité et preste à tomber dans ce qui lui paroissoit le plus grand des malheurs, / 3 qui estoit de laisser voir à M. de Nemours l'inclination qu'elle avoit pour luy. (p. 88: 27-31; P1678, II, 130-31)

Here, the narrator takes up the tale again, assumes a position at a greater distance from the character, and assures an exteriorizing perspective (unit 1). The degree of exteriority and dissociation is underlined in three ways. The absence of any subordinating verb clearly separates this sentence from the preceding series of clauses. In 2, the use of *elle se trouvoit* contrasts in function with *elle trouva* and *elle pensa*. Here, the narrator will tell the reader, without benefit of indirect discourse, what the heroine concluded. Finally, the use of *ce qui lui paroissoit* clearly dissociates narrator and heroine.

In the rest of the passage, it is the objective omniscient narrator who restates and arranges the heroine's reflexions. The moments of closeness to a character's interiority are all the more effective because of their rarity.

The most extended example of these techniques in Part II is the passage dealing with Mme de Clèves's immediate reactions to the lost letter (pp. 96: 28-98: 15; cf. Francillon, pp. 163-66). The experience of jealousy is one of the keys, if not the key, to the heroine's subsequent course of action. This passage may be divided into five movements. In the first section, the narrator remains outside the character and treats her as an object of sympathetic description:

1 Mme de Clèves leut cette lettre et la releut plusieurs fois, sans sçavoir néantmoins ce qu'elle avoit lu: / 2 Elle voyoit seulement que M. de Nemours ne l'aimoit pas comme elle l'avoit pensé, et qu'il en aimoit d'autres qu'il trompoit comme elle. / 3 Quelle vue et quelle connoissance pour une personne de son humeur, qui avoit une passion violente, qui venoit d'en donner des marques à un homme qu'elle en jugeoit indigne, et à un autre qu'elle maltraitoit pour l'amour de luy! / 4 Jamais affliction n'a esté si piquante et si vive: il luy sembloit que ce qui faisoit l'aigreur de cette affliction estoit ce qui s'estoit passé dans cette journée, et que si M. de Nemours n'eust point eu lieu de croire qu'elle l'aimoit, elle ne se fust pas souciée qu'il en eust aimé une autre. / 5 Mais elle se trompoit elle-même; et ce mal, qu'elle trouvoit si insuportable, estoit la jalousie avec toutes les horreurs

dont elle peut estre accompagnée. (pp. 96: 28-97: 8; P1678, II, 168-70)

As in the previous passage, 1 and 2 present a resumé of the heroine's reaction. The only possible touch of affectivity is the triple use of Nemours as the subject of the subordinate clause in 2, the repetition functioning somewhat like the list of particulars in an indictment. Unit 3 and the first independent clause of 4 convey the character's agitation through the narrator's exclamations, although the reader still is supplied with only the essence of the heroine's thoughts. The technique is the same as that used in the first passage studied and has the paradoxical effect both of expressing and controlling irrationality. To exclaim over something is to have an emotional tie with that object, but the clause *pour une personne de son humeur* shows the reader that the narrative voice proceeds from outside the character. The rest of 4 is, of course, the work of the analytic, more than the sympathetic, narrator. The *il lui sembloit* and the two subjunctives make this clear. 5 draws the conclusion, first by tersely restating the fact that Mme de Clèves misjudges her situation, and then in giving the correct name to the emotion. In the second clause of 5, the narrator remains analytical in putting the character's emotions in perspective, while at the same time stating an attitude towards jealousy. The delay in using the term itself (*ce mal* as subject, followed by the adjectival relative containing the affective *insupportable*) foregrounds *la jalousie*. The following superlative *avec toutes les horreurs dont elle peut estre accompagnée* serves to reinforce the statement and indicates the narrator's attitude towards the emotion (12).

In the next section, the heroine's thoughts are presented in much the same way as in units 4 through 9 of the passage just discussed:

1 Elle voyoit par cette lettre, que M. de Nemours avoit une galanterie depuis longtemps. / 2 Elle trouvoit que celle qui avoit écrit la lettre avoit de l'esprit et du mérite; elle lui paroissoit digne d'estre aimée; elle lui trouvoit plus de courage qu'elle ne s'en trouvoit à elle-mesme, et elle envioit la force qu'elle avoit eue de cacher ses sentimens à M. de Nemours. / 3 Elle voyoit, par la fin de la lettre, que cette personne se croyoit aimée; elle pensoit que la discrétion que ce prince luy avoit fait paroître, et dont elle avoit été si touchée, n'estoit peut-estre que l'effet de la passion qu'il avoit

pour cette autre personne à qui il craignoit de déplaire. / 4 Enfin elle pensoit tout ce qui pouvoit augmenter son affliction et son désespoir. / 5 Quels retours ne fit-elle point sur elle-mesme; quelles réflexions sur les conseils que sa mère luy avoit donnez; / 6 combien se repentit-elle de ne s'estre pas opiniâtrée à se séparer du commerce du monde, malgré M. de Clèves, / 7 ou de n'avoir pas suivy la pensée qu'elle avoit eue de luy avouer l'inclination qu'elle avoit pour M. de Nemours? (p. 97: 8-28; P1678, II, 170-73)

The reader passes from the more general statement that Mme de Clèves saw that Nemours had a long-standing affair (1), through the more specific reflexions (2 and 3), to the point where the narrator intervenes to reestablish a distance between reader and character (4). In this section, the series of clauses and sentences beginning with *elle*, rarely connected by coordinating conjunctions, translates the onrush of painful reflexions.

The following rhetorical questions, in units 5 through 7, keep the reader at a distance from the character. Although these questions do illustrate by their form the sympathetic agitation of the narrator, it is the *narrator*'s voice that gives a summary of the character's reactions in a formally emotional way. One of the clearest indices of this paradox is the use of *ou* at the beginning of unit 7. Had *et* been used, the reader would have thought himself in the presence of a sort of list of the character's thoughts. The *ou* not only foregrounds the schematic and rhetorical nature of the procedure but also presents a radical alternative, the *aveu*.

In the ensuing section, the judgmental *trouver* is twice used as the subordinating verb, and the syntax is more complex (hypotaxis as opposed to parataxis):

Elle trouvoit qu'elle auroit mieux fait de la découvrir à un mary dont elle connoissoit la bonté, et qui auroit eu intérêt à la cacher, que de la laisser voir à un homme qui en estoit indigne, qui la trompoit, qui la sacrifioit peut-estre, et qui ne pensoit à estre aimé d'elle, que par un sentiment d'orgueil et de vanité: Enfin, elle trouva que tous les maux qui luy pouvoient arriver, et toutes les extrémitez où elle se pouvoit porter, estoient moindres que d'avoir laissé voir à M. de Nemours qu'elle l'aimoit, et de connoître qu'il en aimoit une autre. Tout ce qui la consoloit estoit de penser au moins, qu'après cette connoissance elle n'avoit plus rien à craindre d'elle-mesme, et qu'elle seroit entièrement guérie de l'inclination qu'elle avoit pour ce prince. (pp. 97: 28-98: 7; P1678, II, 173-75)

The heroine's thoughts are represented in a more highly intellectualized manner than has been the case since the beginning of the passage. The *Enfin, elle trouva* announces the conclusion not only by the adverb, but through the use of the past definite, since all the foregoing verbs of thought (*voir, penser, trouver*) had been in the imperfect. In a similar manner, the verbs in the previous section, when the narrator intervenes (*ne fit-elle point*, p. 97: 22; *se repentit-elle*, p. 97: 24), are in the past definite, conveying the notion that the scene is drawing to a close. The last sentence of the paragraph places the reader farther outside the character, who has become, grammatically as well as in the narrative, the object rather than the subject. The independent clause «Tout ce qui la consoloit estoit de penser au moins» is interesting not only in this way, but also because, while the *au moins* seems to reflect the reality of the heroine's thought breaking through the structure («penser . . . qu'elle n'avoit plus rien a craindre d'elle-mesme, et qu'elle seroit entièrement guérie de l'inclination qu'elle avoit pour ce prince»), it is also ironic since it throws doubt on the accuracy of Mme de Clèves's analysis. A final section (p. 98: 8-15) serves not only as a transition back to the other characters but also removes the reader still further from the character. The narrator's tone has also cooled considerably.

In the rest of Part II and in the beginning of Part III, the reader's attention is turned away from the Princess and centered on the Vidame's story. The techniques of presentation differ in only one respect from the story of Sancerre. This time the reader is given extensive information withheld from Mme de Clèves. Because her jealousy is so crucial to the novel's structure, this shift in point of view is especially effective. The last passage discussed (pp. 97: 8-98: 7) is endowed with retroactive irony, while the heroine's subsequent thoughts and actions, until she learns the truth, acquire dramatic irony. In addition, while the complexity of the Vidame's story tends to demand the reader's entire attention, some tension is created by the heroine's lengthy absence from the stage. The absence seems lengthy because of the complexity of the tale.

In sum, the interior views in Part II, relying on secondary mimesis, have a double function. Using expressionist presentation (13), they provide the reader with material upon which his imagination may build affect (see Nurse, p. 206), thus creating sympathy (in the etymological sense) with the heroine. At the same time, these passages enhance the novel's irony. One of the features of secondary mimesis previously noted was the partial stylization of the irrational. Expressionist presentation implies the intervention of an analytical mind. As a consequence, the form in which interiority is presented maintains a degree of distance between reader and character. Combined with the reader's wider knowledge of other characters' behavior and thoughts, this distance shows Mme de Clèves's interiority in an ironic light. In this irony lies the advantage of art over life, the pleasure of esthetic contemplation.

The presentation of the heroine's interiority through secondary mimesis creates the complementary effects of complicity (imaginative participation) and irony. The reader sees a great deal, but not everything, from the heroine's viewpoint. The varying esthetic distance conditions the reader's perspective. Through secondary mimesis, Mme de Lafayette intensifies the irony and complicity discussed at the end of Chapter I.

The fundamental choice of presenting particular moments of interiority at all is in itself a value judgment (14). The tale's purport is emotion not events (15). The stylization of secondary mimesis may indeed have been motivated by the seventeenth-century penchant for intellectual analysis of the passions (Fabre, «Bienséance et sentiment,» p. 57), and a tempting parallel may be drawn between this motivation and Mme de Clèves's efforts to dominate her feelings (Niderst, p. 172). This latter analogy, however, relies on a dangerous assimilation of author with protagonist. One is on surer ground if the analogy is made between the method of presentation and the code lived by the characters.

The reader is sensitive to the passages of interiority, not only because of what he can add imaginatively, but also because of the ambiance created by the prose. Its restraint—constantly belied by events—parallels, and in large measure creates, for the reader the atmosphere of the characters' society. They live in a world of aprioristically encoded behavior, even in matters of love. The conventions born of *la cortezia* subsisted, although their socio-political basis had long since vanished (16). As a consequence, the forms are constantly violated. Likewise, the characters' passions violate the restraint of the expression used to describe them. In this way, too, secondary mimesis draws the reader into the novel's world.

*Chapter III*


THE CHARACTERS AS ACTORS
SOLILOQUY AND DIALOGUE (TOME III)


One of the most salient characteristics of the third section of *La Princesse de Clèves* is the frequency of soliloquies and scenes in dialogue (1). Here, Mme de Clèves becomes an active rather than passive participant in her own drama. The author's narrative strategy involves not only the passages in direct discourse themselves, but also the choice to present certain material in this form, as well as the manipulation of the surrounding context, making use of the contrast afforded by the juxtaposition of direct speech with the third-person narrative.

Although there are, as before, scenes of interiority constructed with the framing effect, a difference appears. Soliloquies take the place of secondary mimesis. This technique appears initially after the writing of the false letter. Mme de Clèves's regrets are presented in two movements: first with secondary mimesis (pp. 119: 32-121: 14) and then through the use of direct discourse (p. 121: 14-29). The progression from indirect to direct style is, of course, in harmony with the intensified progress of the plot and with the Princess' increasing realization, and admission to herself, of her passion for Nemours (see Francillon, p. 156).

Soliloquy first appears in connection with «les inquiétudes mortelles de la déffiance et de la jalousie» (pp. 120: 35-121: 1). In Part II (pp. 96: 28-97: 8; see above Chapter II), the narrator had already intervened on the subject of jealousy, indicating the important role it plays in the novel. It is thus not surprising that the first soliloquy should appear when Mme de Clèves becomes conscious, not simply of her passion, but of its bond to jealousy, an awareness without which her subsequent behavior would make no sense.

Here is the passage in which the first soliloquy occurs:

1 Elle trouva qu'il estoit presque impossible qu'elle pust estre contente de sa [Nemours's] passion; / 2 mais quand je le pourois estre, disoit-elle, qu'en veux-je faire? / 3 veux-je la souffrir? / 4 veux-je y répondre? / 5 veux-je m'engager dans une galanterie, / 6 veux-je manquer à M. de Clèves, / 7 veux-je me manquer à moy-mesme? / 8 Et veux-je enfin m'exposer aux cruels repentirs et aux mortelles douleurs que donne l'amour? / 9 Je suis vaincue et surmontée par une inclination qui m'entraisne malgré moy: / 10 toutes mes résolutions sont inutilles, / 11 je pensay hier tout ce que je pense aujourd'huy, et je fais aujourd'huy tout le contraire de ce que je résolus hier; / 12 il faut m'aracher de la présence de M. de Nemours; / 13 il faut m'en aller à la campagne, quelque bizarre que puisse paroistre mon voyage; / 14 et si M. de Clèves s'opiniastre à l'empescher ou à en vouloir sçavoir les raisons, peut-estre lui feray-je le mal, et à moy-mesme aussi de les lui aprendre. (p. 121: 13-29; P1678, III, 66-68)

This passage, as is fitting, comes after the presentation of the Princess' interiority, since verbalization, even in solitude, demands a certain amount of control. The heroine's words are structured so that, even here, there is a tension between the violence of the feeling denoted by the use of direct discourse and repetition, and the intellectual control denoted by the progression of the argument.

In the passages of secondary mimesis, the use of indirect discourse made the narrator's mediating presence felt. Here, for the first time, the character's exact statement of her feelings is presented without apparent mediation. The use of repetition conveys the intensity of the emotion. The anaphoric *veux-je* occurs seven times (units 2-8). The following lines (units 9-11) pick up and center around the repetition of *je, me* and *moi,* while the last units (12 and 13) are structured around the two *il faut.*

However, the argument itself unfolds with a rigor which belies the character's agitated state. The reader moves from rhetorical questions (2-8; see Tiefenbrun, pp. 51-52) through a statement of the situation (9-11) to a resolution to act in certain ways (12-14).

The chiasmus «je pensay hier tout ce que je pense aujourd'huy et je fais aujourd'huy tout le contraire de ce que je résolus hier» illustrates the paradoxical nature of the passage. It is a formal device which serves as a summation of the second portion of the argument (9 and 10) and prepares the conclusion (12-14). At the same time, this sentence creates tension, ambiguity and conflict. The whole soliloquy also functions paradoxically, by both releasing and controlling tension.

In the discussion of secondary mimesis, it was noted that this manner of presenting interiority stylized the irrational so as to make it appear rational. The reader was given a clear picture of the character's state through the narrator's mediation. He was given a sense of the emotion involved by an accumulation of the character's reflexions in clauses which, through their often irregular rhythm, also translated that agitation. In the soliloquies, direct discourse, by its formal contrast with the narrative and with indirect discourse, highlights the protagonists' thoughts to a greater degree than secondary mimesis. The obvious mediation of the narrator is absent. The rigorous ordering of the soliloquies, however, reveals the hand of the writer. The presentation of emotion is more direct than in secondary mimesis, but an element of control subsists (cf. Fabre, *L'Art de l'analyse*, p. 40; Niderst, pp. 73-75, 161).

The two other uses of soliloquy in Part III form a sort of diptych in which one sees first Mme de Clèves and then Nemours reacting to the revelation of the *aveu*. In the presentation of the Princess' thoughts (pp. 147: 12-148: 9), the narrator uses a rhetorical question as the transition between the resumé of the character's thoughts (p. 147: 12-19) and the soliloquy (pp. 147: 22-148: 4). The question «Comment excuser une si grande im-

prudence, et qu'estoit devenue l'extrême discrétion de ce prince, dont elle avoit esté si touchée?» (p. 147: 19-21) clearly invites the reader to join the narrator in agreeing with the heroine's view of Nemours. While it could be argued that the question is in free indirect style, the first clause can also be considered a continuation of the *récit*, and, in fact, one of the sort of
interventions typical of the narrator. The use of *ce prince* to refer to Nemours also indicates that it is unlikely that the question is an example of free indirect style, and not narrator intervention (2). By viewing it as a rhetorical question posed by the
narrator, one has an explanation of the effect, which is to enlist
the reader's agreement. The interrogative form foregrounds the
assent given to Mme de Clèves's position. From the formal stand-
point, it smooths the transition to direct discourse, something
more noticeable in the original edition where the entire passage
is part of the same paragraph (III, 183). The framing effect of
the narrator's more general statements at the beginning and end
of the passages dealing with interiority is especially evident here,
since the final statement differs only slightly from the initial
one:

De tous ses maux celuy qui se présentoit à elle avec le plus de violence, estoit d'avoir sujet de se plaindre de M. de Nemours, et de ne trouver aucun
moyen de le justifier. (p. 147: 12-15; P1678, III, 181-82)

mais quelque douleur dont elle se trouvast accablée, elle sentoit bien
qu'elle auroit eu la force de les supporter si elle avoit esté satisfaite de M.
de Nemours. (p. 148: 6-9; P1678, III, 185)

The ensuing passage containing Nemours's regrets (pp. 148:
10-149: 23) is structured in basically the same way as the other
passages of interiority. There is, however, no invitation for the
reader to sympathize with the Duke. The two passages do indeed balance each other, but the rhetorical question in the case
of Mme de Clèves modifies the esthetic distance and combines
with all the previous instances of interiority to keep the reader
inclined in her favor. The foregrounding of Nemours's regrets
gives them special force, thus preventing the Duke from appearing utterly devoid of scruples. If he were pictured as totally
boorish, the reader would be unable to sympathize with the her-

oine's dilemma.

Although there are no other soliloquies in Part III, there are a number of other instances of interiority. After the confession, the narrator gives, serially, resumés of each of the principals' thoughts. In the heroine's case (p. 129: 6-28), the reader is simply told that Mme de Clèves was terrified by what she had done and that she spent the night in uncertainty. Not only does the highly controlled passage serve as a descrescendo after the charged confession scene, it also reflects the temporary state of relative calm and the sense of relief the character feels after her act.

The description of Nemours's state is even briefer and more schematic (pp. 129: 29-130: 17). The narrator does not entirely refrain from commentary. While Nemours «trouva de la gloire à s'être fait aimer d'une femme *si différente de toutes celles de son sexe*» (p. 130: 9-10), the result of his augmented passion is that «il tomba dans une imprudence *assez ordinaire*» (p. 130: 19-20). The juxtaposition diminishes Nemours, especially since his thoughtless behavior follows so closely on the confession scene. The contrasting actions of the two characters make clear to the reader the incommensurability of their values (as acted not enounced), which Mme de Clèves herself will point out in her renunciation (see Woshinsky, p. 114).

As for M. de Clèves, only a resumé of his pains and suspicions (p. 131: 9-22) is offered. The narrator's use of hyperbole («Jamais mary n'avoit eu une passion si violente pour sa femme et ne l'avoit tant estimée,» p. 131: 10-12) puts him on the same plane as his wife, but only through his appreciation of her. His quite natural jealous curiosity shows the reader that he will be incapable of the ideal response for which his wife hoped (3).

The longer portion of the passage deals with the men the Prince suspects. As a result, his «douleur mortelle» (p. 131: 10) has less emotional impact on the reader than the reactions of either Mme de Clèves or Nemours. The plot-function of the Prince's jealousy takes precedence. One is more concerned with the danger of his finding out the truth than with his pain. M. de Clèves's position in the novel has as much potential for evoking interest and sympathy as his wife's. It is manipulation of per-

spective in such passages as this which keeps the novel from becoming «le roman du mari» instead of *La Princesse de Clèves* (4).
In the episode in which M. de Clèves tricks his wife in order to discover the identity of his rival (pp. 133: 29-135: 20), the narrator uses her omniscience to underline the complexities of observation and attempted dissimulation. More interesting, however, are the main scenes of Part III, essentially in dialogue, where the writer limits the narrator's omniscience and manipulates point of view in a somewhat different way than has thus far been the case (5). Near the beginning of the third section of *La Princesse de Clèves*, Nemours comes to explain the origin of the letter to Mme de Clèves. From the end of the description of her reaction to the letter (p. 98: 15), through the Vidame's tale, until Nemours's arrival at the Princess' door, the reader receives no supplementary information about her state and assumes, as the author helpfully points out («Mme de Clèves estoit encore au lit, l'esprit aigri et agité de tristes pensées qu'elle avoit eu [sic] pendant la nuit,» p. 112: 16-18), that her feelings have not changed. The narrator steps away from Mme de Clèves and provides the reader with the conversation as well as with certain insights into Nemours's mental state. The reader not only knows why Mme de Clèves reacts as she does, and that she is in error, but he also watches her betray herself to Nemours, thanks to the narrator's two interjections:

Ce prince ne fut pas blessé de ce refus, une marque de froideur dans un temps où elle pouvoit avoir de la jalousie, n'estoit pas un mauvais augure.
(p. 112: 23-25; P1678, III, 25-26)

L'aigreur que M. de Nemours voyoit dans l'esprit de Mme de Clèves lui donnoit le plus sensible plaisir qu'il eust jamais eu, et balançoit son impatience de se justifier. (pp. 113: 34-114: 2; P1678, III, 32)

The narrator uses Nemours's reactions to underline the transparency of Mme de Clèves's behavior. Unlike many of the previous instances of direct discourse, the reader has the impression here that he hears both sides of the conversation. However, because of his fuller knowledge and the two insights into Nemours, the reader feels that he is observing Mme de Clèves along with Nemours (cf. Francillon, p. 110). Under the impetus of jealousy, the Princess begins to assume a more active role, and the narrator, instead of focusing so much on her perception of events, tends to step back and let the reader, with the other characters, watch her act. There is, of course, somewhat of a return to interiority when Nemours repeats the Vidame's story. What interests the reader is Mme de Clèves's reaction. The narrator, however, observes the heroine's change of mind from a distance. Indeed, the narrator's tone waxes almost sarcastic: «elle ne put s'empêcher de le [the note] prendre, de regarder le dessus pour voir s'il s'adressoit au Vidame de Chartres et de le lire *tout entier*» (p. 115: 4-6). The generalization has the same effect: «et, comme on persuade aisément une vérité agréable, il convainquit Mme de Clèves qu'il n'avoit point de part à cette lettre» (p. 115: 9-11).

With the narrator's assistance, the reader steps back from the heroine. This distancing is ironic. The narrator underlines the change in the Princess' behavior: «enfin si tost qu'elle le crut innocent, elle entra avec un esprit ouvert et tranquille dans les mesmes choses qu'elle sembloit d'abord ne daigner pas entendre» (p. 115: 17-19). Attention is then turned to the scene at the Reine Dauphine's, where again the conversation is not shaped to Mme de Clèves's perspective, but in which, except for the notation of her embarrassment (p. 116: 31-32), the reader remains a spectator.

The Dauphine's comment that only Mme de Clèves would tell her husband all (p. 117: 20-22) is ironic on several levels. There is retroactive irony, for the reader aware of the *aveu*. There is the greater irony that, even during and after the confession, Mme de Clèves never tells her husband everything. Finally, it is ironic that the Reine Dauphine makes her observation, not on the basis of Mme de Clèves's actual behavior (M. de Clèves may have been the one literally to give the letter back, but the sequence of events is not as the Princess describes them here), but rather notes her excessive honesty on the basis of what might well be called a lie.

As for the scene in which the letter is actually forged (pp. 118: 1-119: 31), the author avoids any direct discourse, indirect discourse, or detailed account of the characters' activities. The narrator stands back from the scene in this way because the actual remarks are of less importance than the atmosphere and the attitudes of the characters, and because a detailed description of Mme de Clèves's flirtatious behavior might well provoke in the reader the same sort of condemnation engaged in by the heroine herself (pp. 119: 32-121: 32). Such structuring would destroy the carefully established sense of complicity and sympathy with Mme de Clèves. Not only does the narrator carefully edit the scene, but the sense of distance is increased as well by the disruption of the temporal sequence (p. 119: 14-31) when the ultimate results of the faulty forgery are detailed.

The distancing must not be confused with objectivity. While Mme de Clèves does exhibit complicity in the scene, the narrator points out a subtle difference between her attitude and Nemours's: «Cet air de mystère et de confidence n'estoit pas d'un médiocre charme pour ce prince et *mesme* pour Mme de Clèves» (p. 118: 20-22). It is as though the *mesme* hints at greater initial hesitancy on the Princess' part. Much more important, however, is the absence of any indication of M. de Clèves's actions. This optic is the same as the lovers' solipsistic one. In addition, emphasis on the husband's real, as opposed to formal, presence would risk making the scene too compromising for the heroine, as would have a detailed description of the conversation. Here, as in the treatment of the Prince's reaction to his wife's confession, the author is careful to avoid allowing the reader's interest to fragment.

Studies of dissimulation in *La Princesse de Clèves* point to Nemours's presence during the confession scene as a significant example of the pervasive voyeurism. Examinations of point of view describe the scene's presentation through Nemours's eyes (6). While the scene does indeed form a most important link in the chain of mutual spying in which the principals engage, the question of point of view is another matter.

As the scene opens, the narrator describes Nemours's arrival at Coulommiers and his hiding in the pavilion. The reader is clearly informed that Nemours hears the conversation (p. 123: 2-28). The direct discourse itself has the usual foregrounding effect, but, of course, contains no indication as to whether or not it is filtered through Nemours's consciousness. The first two descriptive interventions, «avec un air embarrassé» (p. 124: 1) and «avec un embarras qui augmentoit toujours» (p. 124: 11-12), can be attributed either to Nemours or to the narrator. The next intervention (p. 124: 21-26) is also indeterminate, although the statement «qui augmentoit toujours la curiosité de son mari» (p. 124: 23-24) leads one to attribute this passage to the omniscient narrator. In the two subsequent cases, the situation is different:

Mme de Clèves ne répondit point; et son silence achevant de confirmer son mari dans ce qu'il avoit pensé . . . (p. 125: 1-3; P1678, III, 82)

M. de Clèves estoit demeuré pendant tout ce discours, la teste appuyée sur ses mains, hors de lui-mesme, et il n'avoit pas songé à faire relever sa femme. Quand elle eut cessé de parler, qu'il jetta les yeux sur elle, qu'il la vid à ses genoux le visage couvert de larmes, et d'une beauté si admirable, il pensa mourir de douleur. (p. 125: 25-30; P1678, III, 85-86)

Here, it is obviously the narrator who relates what the Prince thought, and it is only after the essential part of the scene is over that Nemours's presence is overtly indicated (p. 127: 12-28). The rest of the scene (p. 127: 29-31) can be attributed either to Nemours or the narrator.

Nemours's presence does not modify the way in which the scene is narrated. Indeed, the fact of his presence is expressly ignored by the author in the main body of the scene. Nemours's presence is formal in the sense that it does not modify the structure of the scene, nor does it influence the interpolated descriptive passages. It is, of course, effective in heightening the tension, since the reader knows Nemours is a hidden witness, and the placement of the description of his reactions slightly before the actual end of the scene reminds the reader of this fact. But it would be erroneous to conclude that the reader sees the confession through Nemours's eyes. It is the narrator who points first to Nemours, then to the Princess and her husband, back again to Nemours, and once more to M. and Mme de Clèves. Then the narrator closes the scene (pp. 128: 32-129: 6). Since Mme de Clèves takes here what is as yet her most active role, the narrator gives no interior description of her until the end of the episode, and even then, it is from a certain distance.

Direct discourse again carries the weight of the scene between M. and Mme de Clèves on their return to Paris (pp. 132: 8-133: 11). The initial favorable evaluation of M. de Clèves by the narrator (p. 132: 8-9) reinforces an attitude held by the heroine, and to be shared by the reader, if his orientation is to be largely based on her perspective (7).

In the long scene at the Reine Dauphine's in which Mme de Clèves learns that the *aveu* is known (pp. 137: 34-143: 16), the narrator's interventions focus first on the heroine, then on Nemours, so that the reader appreciates the tension between the two protagonists and between their thoughts and outward conduct. The fact that they are both actors is indicated through the almost equal attention devoted to each. «En lisant cette aventure,» Valincour comments, «l'on entre dans les sentiments de Madame de Clèves; l'on souffre avec elle; et il n'y a rien que l'on ne fît pour la tirer de la peine où l'on se la représente» (8). This is an accurate account of how the descriptions function. The reader, long conditioned to do so, reacts to the Princess' position affectively. The actual descriptions of Nemours, except for the first (p. 140: 17-28), show him in control, trying to produce certain effects on Mme de Clèves. Consequently, the tension involved in the reader's interest in the Princess is increased.

In the description of the subsequent dispute between M. and Mme de Clèves over the revelation of their secret (pp. 143: 24-146: 31), there is, as in the previous scene, a high degree of dramatic irony. In the quarrel, as with the complaints that M. de Clèves had made to the Princess before their marriage (pp. 31: 17-32: 18), the narrator indicates that she provides only the essence of the character's remarks: «ils ne sortirent de ce silence que pour redire les mesmes choses qu'ils avoient déjà dittes plusieurs fois» (p. 145: 33-35). While equal attention is paid to each in the scene itself, the degree of intensity and detail in which the Prince's thoughts are conveyed, is, as always, more limited than in the case of Mme de Clèves, or even Nemours.

A comparison of this conversation with the discussion between the Prince and his fiancée before their marriage (pp. 31:

17-32: 18) shows how the distribution of dialogue has evolved. In the earlier scene, there are twenty-eight lines of dialogue, of which approximately twenty-nine percent are spoken by the heroine. Here, on the contrary, sixty-one percent of the dialogue is spoken by Mme de Clèves. The change in mode of presentation from third-person narrative to dialogue and soliloquy is not only in keeping with the characters' clearer awareness of their positions but also conveys to the reader this increased consciousness and the resulting degree of activity through the direct form taken by the narrative.

In the ensuing passages, the narrator describes, in turn, each of the protagonists' states (pp. 146: 3-149: 23), much as she did after the confession scene. In contrast, the passage immediately preceding, devoted to the Prince's feelings, seems much more distant. The initial acquisition of reader-complicity has both husband and wife as its object: «Il est aisé de s'imaginer en quel estat ils passèrent la nuit» (p. 146: 3-4). The indirect form is used exclusively for M. de Clèves's feelings. The subsequent soliloquies overshadow M. de Clèves's role, once again keeping the novel clearly focused. Part III closes with the description of the tourney and the King's accident. The protagonists' drama continues, but more slowly, and the narrator integrates it into the social drama which takes temporary precedence.

The use of dialogue in the principal scenes in Part III conveys the protagonists' higher degree of consciousness and activity by the very presentation in direct form (9). The soliloquies also contribute to the impression of increased action and awareness.

Functioning in concert with passages of interiority in indirect discourse and with the narrator's interventions, soliloquy and dialogue are two capital elements in the shaping of perspective in Part III. The formal contrasts between the various modes of presentation are sharpened, and this formal tension is an analogue of the intensified progress of the plot.

*Chapter IV*


## FOCUS (TOME IV)


It may seem perverse to choose the last section of *La Princesse de Clèves* as the principal field for study of the novel's focus. Both M. de Clèves and Nemours here receive more attention than in any of the preceding parts of the book (cf. Francillon, pp. 112-14). Indeed, the heroine seems partially eclipsed in the passages which precede the Prince's death. In the rest of the novel, the reader's attention has rarely been so much occupied by either of the other two principals. What then is the effect of this shifted focus on the reader's larger vision of the novel?

Here is the first passage in Part IV dealing with the protagonists:

Quoy que ce fût une chose fâcheuse pour M. de Clèves de ne pas conduire Mme Elizabeth, néantmoins il ne put s'en plaindre par la grandeur de celuy qu'on luy préféroit; mais il regrettoit moins cet employ par l'honneur qu'il en eust receu, que parce que c'estoit une chose qui éloignoit sa femme de la cour, sans qu'il parust qu'il eust dessein de l'en éloigner.

Peu de jours après la mort du Roy, on résolut d'aller à Reims pour le sacre. Sitost qu'on parla de ce voyage, Mme de Clèves, qui avoit toujours demeuré chez elle, feignant d'estre malade, pria son mary de trouver bon qu'elle ne suivist point la cour et qu'elle s'en allast à Colomiers prendre l'air et songer à sa santé. Il lui répondit qu'il ne vouloit point pénétrer si c'estoit la raison de sa santé qui l'obligeoit à ne pas faire le voyage, mais qu'il consentoit qu'elle ne le fist point. Il n'eut pas de peine à consentir à une chose qu'il avoit déjà résolue: quelque bonne opinion qu'il eust de la vertu de sa femme, il voyoit bien que la prudence ne vouloit pas qu'il l'exposast plus longtemps à la veue d'un homme qu'elle aimoit. (pp. 157: 34-158: 19; P1678, IV, 11-14)

The Prince's thoughts are summarized by the narrator, but this indirection does not obscure the fact that the reader's attention is focused on M. de Clèves as he is further informed of the extent of the Prince's jealousy. The heroine is seen only from the outside, much as her husband would see her. Mme de Lafayette's use of *la prudence* in the concluding statement is heavily ironic. The Prince was after all initially distinguished by «une prudence qui ne se trouve guères avec la jeunesse» (p. 10: 1-2). Now this same *prudence* serves in part as a mask interposed by the Prince between himself and his jealousy, and it is this same jealousy which will make him, most imprudently, hear only part of his spy's report (pp. 174: 20-175: 2; see Francillon, pp. 146, 150).

The reader's attention is briefly diverted to Nemours's abortive attempt to see Mme de Clèves, an incident which provokes the first really explicit explosion of the Prince's jealousy (pp. 160: 2-162: 28). The passage may be divided into three parts. First, the narrator describes M. de Clèves's initial reaction:

1 Ces paroles qu'elles croyoient si indifférentes, ne l'estoient pas pour M. de Clèves, quoyqu'il deust bien s'imaginer que M. de Nemours pouvoit trouver souvent des occasions de parler à sa femme. / 2 Néantmoins la pensée qu'il estoit chez elle, qu'il y estoit seul, et qu'il luy pouvoit parler de son amour, / 3 luy parut dans ce moment une chose si nouvelle et si insupportable, que la jalousie s'alluma dans son cœur avec plus de violence qu'elle n'avoit encore fait. / 4 Il luy fut impossible de demeurer chez la Reine, il s'en revint, ne sçachant pas mesme pourquoy il revenoit, et s'il avoit dessein d'aller interrompre M. de Nemours. / 5 Sitost qu'il approcha de chez luy, il regarda s'il ne verroit rien qui luy pust faire juger si ce prince y estoit encore: il sentit du soulagement en voyant qu'il n'y estoit plus, et il trouva de la douceur à penser qu'il ne pouvoit y avoir demeuré longtemps. Il s'imagina que ce n'estoit peut-estre pas M. de Nemours, dont il devoit estre jaloux: / 6 Et quoy qu'il n'en doutast point, il cherchoit à en

douter; mais tant de choses l'en auroient persuadé, qu'il ne demeuroit pas longtemps dans cette incertitude qu'il désiroit. (pp. 159: 31-160: 21; P1678, IV, 20-22)

With the exception of unit 2, in which the triplication of *qu'il* and the increasing precision of the imagined scene convey the character's agitation, there is no secondary mimesis in this description. The narrator summarizes the Prince's reactions, and the reader is told of the conflict rather than shown it.

The second section of the passage (p. 160: 21-33) contains the narrator's summary of the initial part of the conversation between husband and wife. There are only two descriptive notes in this resumé. The Prince asks his wife «en tremblant» if she has seen anyone other than those she has named (p. 160: 27). When she denies this, the transition to direct discourse reads: «M. de Clèves reprenant la parole avec un ton qui marquoit son affliction» (p. 160: 31-32). Attention is thus kept centered on the Prince.

The third part of the passage contains the rest of the dispute between husband and wife, now in direct discourse (pp. 160: 33-162: 28). The transition from indirect to direct presentation occurs when the Prince asks, «Et Monsieur de Nemours . . . ne l'avez-vous point vu ou l'avez-vous oublié?» (p. 160: 33-34). The portion of the conversation given relief by virtue of its being the first statement in direct form is that one which strikes Mme de Clèves most forcefully. This is also the point at which the conversation turns into a dispute. The transition to direct discourse is consonant with M. de Clèves's transition from cautious questioning of his wife to open reproaches, ending with his comment «Je vous demande seulement de vous souvenir que vous m'avez rendu le plus malheureux homme du monde» (p. 162: 27-28).

Through his jealousy the Prince becomes interesting; his conflict could overshadow that of the Princess. Consequently, its direct expression is relegated almost entirely to the last part of the novel, where it serves the important function of laying some of the foundation for the renunciation scene (cf. Francillon's treatment of the Prince, pp. 145-51).

Lest M. de Clèves, even here, eclipse the Princess, this scene is followed almost immediately by an even more powerful one, the night scene at Coulommiers. The reader is not permitted to think as much about M. de Clèves's pain as about its results (the presence of the spy).

The scene between M. de Clèves and his spy is shaped in a somewhat different way. The section in direct discourse (p. 174: 25-35) is characterized by dramatic irony since the reader knows exactly what did happen. The irony operates on two levels. On the one hand, M. de Clèves jumps to conclusions. On the other, the actual events observed by Nemours would, if known, be just as much a confirmation of the Prince's worst fears as an actual rendezvous. The description of the husband's reaction is marked by a certain attenuation: «Il n'y en a peut-estre jamais eu un [désespoir] plus violent, et peu d'hommes d'un aussi grand courage et d'un cœur aussi passionné que M. de Clèves, ont ressenti en mesme temps la douleur que cause l'infidélité d'une maistresse et la honte d'estre trompé par une femme» (p. 175: 2-7; P1678, IV, 89-90). The *peut-estre* and the *peu d'hommes* are used to avoid hyperbole (1). The absence of an absolute judgment here, as well as of any detailed description of the Prince's state, keeps the reader at a certain distance from the character (2). The final explosion of M. de Clèves's désespair is reserved for the scene in direct discourse (pp. 176: 20-179: 16), where the reader sees the Prince interact with his wife; there the novelist avoids the devotion of any exclusive attention to the Prince alone. Although M. de Clèves dominates the scene, he is not the sole object of attention.

One of the two predominant influences in Mme de Clèves's life is her own experience of jealousy and her comprehension of the essential incommensurability of her concept of love with Nemours's. Through his jealousy and death, the Prince becomes the second major influence on his wife (cf. Francillon, pp. 147-48). For this reason, he plays his principal role in Part IV, and, thus, the fundamental perspective of the novel remains intact.

The increased attention paid the Prince in Part IV is balanced by that accorded Nemours. Mme de Clèves's lover is the least interesting of the three protagonists. His problems are essentially tactical, not emotional or moral (3). While he must be made to seem worthy of Mme de Clèves, his limitations must also be evident, since they play a large part in influencing the reader to view experience as the heroine does (cf. Francillon, pp. 151-57). Early in Part IV, Nemours attempts to visit Mme de Clèves (pp. 158: 20-159: 24); the Princess' reaction is one of conflict:

La crainte qu'elle eut qu'il ne luy parlast de sa passion, l'appréhension de luy répondre trop favorablement, l'inquiétude que cette visite pouvoit donner à son mary, la peine de luy en rendre compte, ou de luy cacher toutes ces choses, se présentèrent en un moment à son esprit, et luy firent un si grand embarras, qu'elle prit la résolution d'éviter la chose du monde qu'elle souhaitoit peut-estre le plus. (pp. 158: 30-159: 6; P1678, IV, 15-16)

A few lines later (p. 159: 19-24), Mme de Clèves regrets her action and forgets all the reasons for which she refused to see Nemours. In contrast, the Duke's emotions are less interesting. This is due both to the situation (he is without conflict) and the presentation. The various elements of Mme de Clèves's state are analyzed, and, in this passage, the relationship between imposed analysis and the character's thoughts is particularly clear. The substantives naming the emotions represent the analysis. The contrast between «La crainte qu'elle eut qu'il ne luy parlast de sa passion» and *elle craignoit qu'il ne luy parlast de sa passion* makes clear the additional intellectual step represented by the substantives. The clauses modifying each substantive come much closer to representing the Princess' actual thoughts. The analysis gives concrete form to these thoughts and presents to the reader their cumulative function in the heroine. This passage once more bears out Nurse's understanding (p. 206) of the presentation of emotions.

The description of Nemours's feelings is much more schematic. In fact, all concrete description is avoided:

Il monta avec une agitation et un trouble, qui ne se peut comparer qu'à ceceluy qu'eut Mme de Clèves, quand on luy dit que M. de Nemours venoit pour la voir. (p. 158: 27-30; P1678, IV, 15)

Quelle douleur pour ce prince de ne pas voir Mme de Clèves, et de ne la pas voir parce qu'elle ne vouloit pas qu'il la vist! (p. 159: 10-12; P1678, IV, 17) enfin il s'en alloit avec tout ce qui peut aigrir une vive douleur. (p. 159: 17-18; P1678, IV, 18)

While the reader is not permitted to doubt either the sincerity or the intensity of Nemours's disappointment (conscious insincerity on his part would make Mme de Clèves appear guilty of bad judgment), there is nothing particularly individual or noteworthy about his feelings (4).

When Nemours next appears, he has decided to go to Coulommiers (p. 165: 15-30). In this scene, the narrator juxtaposes Nemours's plan and M. de Clèves's suspicions with this comment: the Prince «ne se trompoit pas dans ses soupçons» (p. 165: 25-26). The narrator once again focuses attention on a character in emotional conflict (here the Prince) rather than on Nemours.

Like the Duke's problem, Mme de Lafayette's use of his presence in the pavilion scene is also tactical. The voyeurism motif achieves greatest ironic subtlety here, when the Prince's man observes Nemours (p. 166: 11-28), who in turn observes Mme de Clèves (pp. 166: 28-167: 21) (5). If there is ever a moment in the novel when the Princess is shown not just giving in to, but indulging in her passion, it is here. As Kaps has observed,

The narrator's privilege is limited to the perspective of an onlooker—the perspective of M. de Nemours. All we know of Mme de Clèves' emotions is what is reflected in her demeanor, what is visible to an observer . . . In this case, the distance which results between the heroine and the reader serves to attenuate our perception of guilt or responsibility on her part. The question of advertence and consent is not raised. All our attention is focused rather on M. de Nemours, through whose eyes we view the entire scene and in whose reactions we are primarily interested. (pp. 52-53)

To say that «primary» interest lies with Nemours is perhaps an overstatement. By this point in the novel, the reader looks first and foremost for evidence of Mme de Clèves's state. The scene itself is preceded by the spying episode, cut by the interjected description of Nemours's reactions (pp. 167: 22-168: 25), and followed by the Duke's lyric effusion (pp. 169: 19-171: 13). It is not that the reader is primarily interested in Nemours, but rather that the author denies him access to the heroine and gives him only one interpretation of her behavior, Nemours's, which he sees as somewhat unreliable because the Duke is in love. Nemours's passion screens Mme de Clèves's. Consequently, the reader's perception of the heroine's complicity is diminished (6).

In the pavilion scene the «tactical» side of Nemours's concerns is played down. It is the genuineness of his passion which is underlined in the descriptions of his indecision about trying to speak to Mme de Clèves (pp. 167: 22-168: 25). Secondary mimesis, belying the initial «On ne peut exprimer ce que sentit M. de Nemours dans ce moment» (p. 167: 22-23), is used to show the violence of his emotion. After he leaves the pavilion, Nemours's soliloquy (pp. 170: 14-171: 13), with its repeated interrogations, serves the function of further highlighting the Duke's passion. His sincerity is juxtaposed with the Princess' complicity, partially justifying the latter. In addition, the use of soliloquy, secondary mimesis, and hyperbole overshadows the passages directly describing her behavior (cf. Kaps, pp. 52-53).

In the rest of Part IV, Nemours appears in a less flattering light, and it is the calculating aspect of his passion which is foregrounded. His thoughts on M. de Clèves's illness (pp. 175: 26-176: 5) show him at his worst (7). Similarly, the account of his discovery of the spy's report and his ensuing calculations (p. 180: 4-32) is inserted in the description of the Princess' grief. This juxtaposition of the two characters' reactions is also unflattering to Nemours. In this passage, however, the narrator feigns lack of omniscience through the use of *peut-estre*, thereby avoiding stating too directly that, even in Mme de Clèves's extreme grief, Nemours has not become indifferent to her: «*Peut-estre* que ces ordres si exacts estoient donnez en veue de ce prince, et pour ne point entendre parler de luy» (p. 180: 26-28). The effect of the litotes is to draw the reader's attention to this fact discreetly (8).

It is at approximately this point that the focus shifts back to Mme de Clèves. In the last passage cited in the preceding paragraph, she is seen from the outside, as she has been almost exclusively in Part IV. Having confessed her passion to her husband, Mme de Clèves's emotions are subject to exterior pressure, such as the discovery that the *aveu* is known, Nemours's attempts to see her, or the Prince's efforts to learn her lover's identity. Her feelings do not really evolve. Thus the reader sees more of the two characters whose actions influence Mme de Clèves (see Niderst, p. 61). It is only after her husband's death that the Princess' feelings evolve and she is again forced into action. This situation is reflected in the treatment not only of the Prince, but also of Nemours. His decision to force an interview (p. 185: 12-28) contains evidence, not only of the exceptional nature of his passion («Est-il possible que l'amour m'ait si absolument osté la raison et la hardiesse et qu'il m'ait rendu si différent de ce que j'ay esté dans les autres passions de ma vie?» p. 185: 17-20), but also of his inability to conceive that she might refuse him («elle est libre, elle n'a plus de devoir à m'opposer,» p. 185: 15-16).

Nemours's role in the renunciation scene itself, and in the last pages of the novel, is intimately connected to the Prince's death and its effect on Mme de Clèves. Her initial grief is presented through a variation of the usual combination of resumé, secondary mimesis, and the *indicible*. First, she is seen from the outside, the object of others' care (p. 179: 22-27). Then, an analysis of her first, emerging rational thoughts is presented:

Quand elle commença d'avoir la force de l'envisager [sa douleur], et qu'elle vid quel mary elle avoit perdu, qu'elle considéra qu'elle estoit la cause de sa mort, et que c'estoit par la passion qu'elle avoit eue pour un autre, qu'elle en estoit cause; l'horreur qu'elle eut pour elle-mesme, et pour M. de Nemours, ne se peut représenter. (pp. 179: 27-180: 3; P1678, IV, 111-12)

The usual immediate contradiction of the *indicible* is delayed by the intercalated passage concerning Nemours. The juxtaposition is ironic. Instead of using the *indicible* either to open or close a passage of interiority, as has previously been the case, the narrator, by turning her attention to Nemours (p. 180: 4-32), leaves the reader in suspense, making the violence of Mme de Clèves's feelings seem all the greater.

When the narrator turns her attention back from Nemours to the heroine, one reads:

La douleur de cette princesse passoit les bornes de la raison; Ce mary mourant, et mourant à cause d'elle et avec tant de tendresse pour elle, ne luy
sortoit point de l'esprit. Elle repassoit incessamment tout ce qu'elle luy
devoit, / 1 et elle se faisoit un crime de n'avoir pas eu de la passion pour
luy, comme si c'eust esté une chose qui eust esté en son pouvoir. / Elle ne
trouvoit de consolation qu'à penser qu'elle le regrettoit autant qu'il méri-
toit d'estre regretté, et qu'elle ne feroit dans le reste de sa vie que ce qu'il
auroit esté bien aise qu'elle eust fait s'il avoit vescu.
    Elle avoit pensé plusieurs fois comment il avoit sceu que M. de Nemours
estoit venu à Colomiers; Elle ne soupçonnoit pas ce prince de l'avoir conté,
et il luy paroissoit mesme indifférent qu'il l'eust redit, tant elle se croyoit
guérie et éloignée de la passion qu'elle avoit eue pour luy. Elle sentoit
néanmoins une douleur vive de s'imaginer qu'il estoit cause de la mort de
son mary, et elle se souvenoit avec peine de la crainte que M. de Clèves luy
avoit témoignée en mourant qu'elle ne l'épousast; / 2 Mais toutes ces douleurs se confondoient dans celle de la perte de son mary, et elle croyoit
n'en avoir point d'autre. (pp. 180: 33-181: 20; P1678, IV, 116-19)

The narrator twice steps totally outside the character's consciousness. In unit 1 she again underlines Mme de Clèves's innocence. The choice of tense does the justifying, while the grammatically unnecessary repetition emphasizes it (see Kaps, p. 52;
Tiefenbrun, «The Art,» p. 44). In unit 2, the narrator intervenes
to create the dramatic irony of Mme de Clèves's assumption
that she mourns only her husband. A parallel can be drawn between this illusion and the illusory suspension of emotions that
Mme de Clèves felt after her mother's death (p. 70: 18-22) (9).
    In the subsequent passages, direct discourse is used to mime
the Princess' increased attention to statements dealing with Nemours (pp. 181: 32-182: 2; 182: 17-21). The resurgence of her
passion is presented through resumé, secondary mimesis, and
exclamations (pp. 183: 24-184: 31) which strike the reader as
more intense than the subsequent reflexions on her duty (p.
184: 11-31). Here again, the narrator steps entirely outside the
character to underscore the dichotomy between the heroine's
passion and her resolutions (pp. 184: 32-185: 2). The rapid distancing which takes place after the renunciation scene is already
begun here. While the narrator has often commented fairly explicitly on the heroine's situation, she has never spoken quite so
directly as here: Mme de Clèves's heart «demeuroit attaché à M.
de Nemours avec une violence qui la mettoit dans un estat digne

de compassion» (p. 184: 33-35). From this point on, there are no more real passages of interiority. Mme de Clèves's state is confirmed by a gesture, her going immediately to the window the next morning (p. 185: 2-7). This is the last time that the reader sees her before the renunciation. The evidence of her continued passion is one of the implicit directions given the reader. Mme de Clèves's decision must be seen as the result of struggle rather than rigidity.

In the renunciation scene itself, the Princess, finally free to avow her love, does so only to refuse it (10). It is ironic that in the main scenes the direct discourse foregrounds not communication, but its impossibility (11). Although the reader is in the position of spectator, his degree of involvement is very great since the silence between the lovers is finally broken.

There is almost no narrator intervention save for the *inquit*(s). In those cases where the intervention is slightly more extensive, it is limited to some physical detail intended to give additional evidence of the characters' emotional state: «En prononçant ces paroles, elle voulut s'en aller; Et M. de Nemours la retenant» (p. 186: 34-35; P1678, IV, 144); «Mme de Clèves . . . le regardant avec des yeux pleins de douceur et de charmes» (p. 187: 8-10; P1678, IV, 145-46); «répondit Mme de Clèves, en s'asseyant» (p. 187: 27; P1678, IV, 148; see Brody, p. 127); «luy dit M. de Nemours, en se jettant à ses genoux» (p. 189: 10-11; P1678, IV, 155); «luy répondit-elle en souriant» (p. 189: 13-14; P1678, IV, 155); «M. de Nemours se jeta à ses pieds, et s'abandonna à tous les divers mouvemens dont il estoit agité; Il luy fit voir, et par ses paroles et par ses pleurs, la plus vive et la plus tendre passion dont un cœur ait jamais été touché. Celuy de Mme de Clèves n'estoit pas insensible, et regardant ce prince avec des yeux un peu grossis par les larmes» (p. 194: 21-27; P1678, IV, 178-79). Each of these gestures correlates with a statement in direct discourse. When Mme de Clèves delivers the main body of her renunciation (pp. 191: 22-194: 20), the narrator refrains from giving any such indications which might dilute the intensity of the scene.

Once, near the very beginning of the scene, the narrator intervenes to continue the exculpation of the heroine, which had been begun through focusing on Nemours in the pavilion scene. The fact that here, for the first time, Mme de Clèves intentionally allows herself to express her love for Nemours would be obvious to the reader even without the intervention: «Mme de Clèves céda pour la première fois au panchant qu'elle avoit pour M. de Nemours» (p. 187: 8-9). It serves to underline the fact that this is the first time the heroine has consciously confronted her passion.

Twice during the scene, resumé is substituted for direct discourse, once to avoid repetition of how Nemours knew of the *aveu* (p. 188: 22-24, 30-31), and again to summarize Nemours's repeated pleas (p. 194: 21-27). The Duke's arguments appear in direct discourse in the preceding passages. Repeating them would evoke less interest than does the description, as it offers a change in perspective, presenting Nemours through the narrator's eyes. Further, a more detailed presentation of the Duke's reasoning might very well make him appear unworthy of Mme de Clèves (12), while the elliptical «la plus vive et la plus tendre passion dont un cœur ait jamais été touché» (p. 194: 23-25; P1678, IV, 178) allows the reader to share the Princess' view (cf. Niderst, p. 158). This is important, for, although the distancing process will accelerate after this last scene, the final steps in the evolution of the heroine's passion, while not presented in detail, depend, for their impact, on the fact that Mme de Clèves's decision is much less final than she here attempts to make it appear.

In the last pages of the novel a counterpoint is established between the ever more distant descriptions of the heroine and Nemours's efforts to destroy her resolutions. The presentation of the Princess' struggles becomes more and more schematic. After her illness, while her conclusions are presented, the final struggle is reduced to the terse observation: «Il se passa un assez grand combat en elle-mesme» (p. 199: 27).

The final distancing serves as a correlative to the distance that Mme de Clèves at last achieves from her passion. Her gradual detachment is evidenced by the presence of generalization in her reflexions: «comme elle connoissoit ce que peuvent les occasions sur les résolutions les plus sages, elle ne voulut pas s'exposer à détruire les siennes, ny revenir dans les lieux où estoit ce qu'elle avoit aimé» (p. 200: 6-9). It is the nature of love to believe itself unique. Never had the Princess' thoughts allowed that to share a common fate or feeling with others was anything but a degradation: «Je seray bientost regardée de tout le monde comme une personne qui a une folle et violente passion» (pp. 147: 35-148: 1). Once she stands physically and morally at least partly outside her passion, Mme de Clèves is able to see her feelings in the context of that *sagesse des nations* of which this generalization is a part.

Distance is also achieved through the anonymous intermediary who speaks to Nemours (pp. 200: 24-201: 7). The message is transmitted through the double screen of this «personne de mérite» (p. 200: 24) and the use of indirect discourse. The telescoping of time, «Enfin, des années entières s'estant passées» (p. 201: 14-15), adds to the distancing effect. With the end of his passion, Nemours disappears, and attention fastens lastly on Mme de Clèves alone:

Elle passoit une partie de l'année dans cette maison religieuse, et l'autre chez elle, mais dans une retraite et dans des occupations plus saintes que celles des couvents les plus austères; et sa vie, qui fut assez courte, laissa des exemples de vertu inimitables. (p. 201: 18-23; P1678, IV, 213)

The narrator stands at a distance and in one final statement capsulizes the last years of the heroine's life, as well as her death. The end of the Princess' struggle is translated by the sentence's almost uniform rhythm, broken only by the relative «qui fut assez courte» which cuts the clause as death cuts off Mme de Clèves's life. The use of religious vocabulary (*maison religieuse, retraite*, des occupations plus *saintes* que celles des *couvents* les plus *austères*, des exemples de *vertu* inimitables) indicates the moral level on which the reader is to view Mme de Clèves's life. The adjective *saintes* is used here for the only time in the novel. This vocabulary is all the more striking because of the complete absence of any mention of religion in the novel (cf. Francillon, pp. 177-79).

Yet even in this final laudatory passage, care is taken to focus the reader's attention with a great deal of precision. The narrator does not say that Mme de Clèves is of inimitable virtue, but rather that her *life* left inimitable *examples* of virtue. Not only would such a categorical statement have alienated the reader, it would have been untrue. This instance, added to previous analyses, underlines the precision of the construction of *La Princesse de Clèves*, where the reader's perspective is carefully shaped to complicity and irony.

# PART II

## LEXICAL PROBLEMS: Irony and Description

A pity beyond all telling
Is hid in the heart of love

W.B. Yeats

# INTRODUCTION

The language of *La Princesse de Clèves*, often referred to as abstract, conventional, or formal, has been assumed to be inadequate to the author's needs (1). This assumption in turn becomes a pretext for reading many things into the novel.

Human psychology has undoubtedly changed but little in the past three hundred years, but our understanding of it, reflected in the proliferation of quasi-scientific terminology in ordinary speech, differs quite radically, for example, from Descartes's *Les Passions de l'âme*. The relation between human psychology and psychological language, and indeed language in general, is not a simple one. While it is true that we experience states which have no names, our major experience of «reality» is intimately related to our ability to account for it in words; the ability to name implies the ability to control, and the unnamed, especially in a society which made fetishes of anatomies of the human heart and of rationality, has quite a different status from the named.

Mme de Lafayette not only acknowledges the limits of language but also extends them. The difficulties in knowing reality and in communication, archetypally illustrated by court life, form an analogue to the problems posed by the limits of language in general. It is quite pointless, however, to assume that *La Princesse de Clèves* would have read more easily had its author but been possessed of present-day French.

The discussion of perspective was based on the belief that the ways in which fictional experience is presented to the reader determine his attitude toward it. Similarly, at the center of the lexical problem is perception. At the level of language, I will be concerned with specific word groups, ironic lexical patternings, and attenuation and description or, more precisely, with what the modern reader perceives as a «lack» of description in *La Princesse de Clèves* (2).

*Chapter I*

## IRONIC STRUCTURES: REALITY

1. Verbs of Perception

While the recurrent use of *paraître, sembler, cacher, voir, regarder* has justly been seized upon by most students of the novel as an indication of the problematic nature of communication at the court (1), little attention has been devoted to the analogous and equally significant question of the reader's perception of this problem.

Taking *paraître* as an example (2), one finds that it is used in three ways: in a purely literal sense, in an ironic sense, and as a subordinating verb for indirect discourse (i.e. impersonal *il parut* and indirect object). As instances of the first of these usages, «les couleurs et les chiffres de Mme de Valentinois *paraissoient* par tout» (p. 5: 13-14) or «Il *parut* alors une beauté à la cour» (p. 17: 1) illustrate the court's emphasis on exterior form and create no immediate problems of comprehension (3). The verb may be used in contexts, however, where its connotation varies according to the supplementary information provided: e.g. the jewel merchant's home which «*paroissoit* plutost celle d'un grand Seigneur que d'un marchand» (p. 18: 29-30).

Because *il lui parut* is also used to introduce indirect discourse, ironic overtones may impinge on the reader's perception of the subordinated material. When describing the encounter at the jeweler's, Mme de Lafayette writes of M. de Clèves: «*il
luy parut* mesme qu'il estoit cause qu'elle avoit de l'impatience
de s'en aller» (p. 19: 17-19). This use of the expression is fully
consonant with the technique of presenting the heroine, at first,
entirely from the outside. As the novel progresses, however, the
constant emphasis on observation and deception, both of self
and of others, adds ironic connotations to the locution. When
Mme de Lafayette writes, for example, that after Nemours's
theft of the portrait, the Princess sees herself as «preste à tomber dans ce qui lui *paroissoit* le plus grand des malheurs, qui estoit de laisser voir à M. de Nemours l'inclination qu'elle avoit
pour luy» (p. 88: 28-31), the choice of verb makes it clear that
the heroine's perception is at least open to question.

Much of the story of *La Princesse de Clèves* is told through
the use of verbs of thought followed by subordinate clauses.
Verbs such as *penser, croire, trouver* and locutions such as *il lui
parut* or *il lui sembla* are used to present both correct and incor-
rect perceptions on the part of the characters. The predomi-
nance of this language suggests a perspective on reality and a
judgment on the nature of *all* perceptions in this novelistic uni-
verse. The language mirrors the uncertainty which so plagues
the characters, leaving all perceptions open to question. For the
reader, the novel has limits which experience lacks. In his eyes,
the repeated use of these verbs constitutes an ironic comment
on perception.

## 2. *Vérité*

It is true that such observations as these might apply to any
number of psychological novels in which more than one character's subjectivity is explored. In *La Princesse de Clèves*, however, the problem of perception is reflected so variously as to
constitute a pervasive theme. The cluster of words having to do

with notions of truth and authenticity (*vrai, vraisemblable, vrai-semblance, vérité, véritablement*) offers some striking examples. The noun *vérité* (4), for example, appears twenty-nine times in the novel. Its first use concerns Guise's view of the initial meeting between Mme de Clèves and Nemours: «soit qu'en effet il eust paru quelque trouble sur son [Mme de Clèves's] visage, ou que la jalousie fist voir au Chevalier de Guise au delà de la *vérité*, il crut qu'elle avoit esté touchée de la veue de ce prince» (p. 37: 7-10). Here the narrator feigns limited knowledge, a stance consonant both with the presentation of the heroine from the exterior and Mme de Clèves's own lack of conscious comprehension of the *coup de foudre*. In any event, the first appearance of *vérité* is in a context of uncertainty and doubt. The reader has been told that, when being introduced to Nemours, the Princess «paroissoit un peu embarassée» (p. 36: 27); whatever Guise may have seen in addition—or thought he had seen—is left undefined. The narrator's alternative explanations of Guise's inference («quelque trouble sur son visage» or «la jalousie fist voir au Chevalier de Guise au delà de la vérité») not only suggest that emotion distorts perception but also leave the reader uncertain as to whether Guise's conclusion was a lucky guess or based on real evidence (5).

When Mme de Chartres informs her daughter that she is wrong about the relationship between the Queen and Montmorency («Vous aviez une opinion bien opposée à la *vérité*,» p. 39: 24) and then makes her famous explanatory statement («ce qui paroist n'est presque jamais la *vérité*,» p. 40: 2), the second mechanism undermining truth is set in motion. The dissimulations of court life remove all criteria by which one may ascertain the truth. A final example underscores the distorting relationship between truth and emotion (the first undermining mechanism): Mlle de Pisseleu's claim to have been born on the day of Diane's marriage, Mme de Chartres explains, was owed to hatred: «la haine le lui faisoit dire, et non pas la *vérité*» (p. 40: 27-28). Once again, an emotion as subject of causal *faire* expresses the absence of «truth.» These are the two basic ironic structures involving *vérité*. In subsequent occurrences (6), the word is most often associated with terms of appearance, deception, or knowledge (7).

In addition to Mme de Chartres's distinction between truth and appearance, the novel contains two more generalizations about truth, both by the narrator: «on persuade aisément une *vérité* agréable» (p. 115: 9-10); «la *vérité* se persuade si aisément lors mesme qu'elle n'est pas vraysemblable» (p. 179: 4-5). These two statements present contradictory pictures of truth. In the first statement, the narrator comments on the heroine's reaction to Nemours's explanation of the lost letter. She emphasizes Mme de Clèves's desire to believe (emotional distortion). In the second case, the narrator explains that the Prince believed his wife's explanation of the events at Coulommiers because she spoke with great assurance (p. 179: 3-4) and because of the intrinsic value attributed to truth (8). The same assumption underlies a number of other occurrences of the noun which concern the heroine. On the first level, there is the character's assumption of the value and efficacy of truth. In one of her early attempts to avoid Nemours, Mme de Clèves thinks of alleging Nemours's rumored love for her. She does not do so, not only because she cannot bring herself to name Nemours, but also because «Elle sentit . . . de la honte de se vouloir servir d'une fausse raison et de déguiser la *vérité* à un homme qui avoit si bonne opinion d'elle» (p. 79: 17-19). In the confession scene, the Princess says: «il faut plus de courage pour avouer cette *vérité* que pour entreprendre de la cacher» (p. 127: 10-11). By pointing up the difference between her choice of confession and customary social behavior, the heroine again places intrinsic value on truth. Her final, somewhat desperate affirmation of faith in truth comes in the interview with her dying husband: «il est impossible qu'avec tant de *vérité*, je ne vous persuade de mon innocence» (p. 178: 22-24). This statement is followed closely by the narrator's generalization: «la *vérité* se persuade si aisément lors mesme qu'elle n'est pas vraysemblable» (p. 179: 4-5). This same sort of approbation of the heroine's behavior is seen in an earlier explanation of why her letter to her husband, written after the argument over Nemours's attempted visit, succeeds in calming M. de Clèves: «comme ses assurances estoient fondées sur la *vérité* et que c'étoit en effet ses sentimens, cette lettre fit de l'impression sur M. de Clèves et luy donna quelque calme» (pp. 162: 34-163: 2).

A number of distinctions must be made. In the heroine's last statement to her husband—«il est impossible qu'avec tant de *vérité* je ne vous persuade de mon innocence» (p. 178: 22-24)—the expression *tant de vérité* deserves scrutiny. As she has learned from the results of her confession, truth is not a simple entity. Unlike the approving narrator, Mme de Clèves cannot be secure in the belief that *la vérité* will disculpate her. Truth has become quantifiable (9), and it is through quantity more than quality that she seeks to persuade. The failure of truth is inevitable from the outset because of the emotions involved, and it is illustrated by the use of the substantive *vérité* in the context of emotional distortion. The word does not reappear after M. de Clèves's death (10). There are no more real secrets. Truth has proved ineffective as a defense against the ravages of passion.

In the novel's world, appearances of passion may not indicate the existence of real feeling. The language of love is cliché-ridden; its inadequacy is itself a cliché. As a consequence, the characters and narrator alike often find it necessary to insist upon the authenticity of feelings. In one third of its occurrences *véritable* is in fact used in this way (11), as when the narrator affirms the sincerity of Nemours's passion: «Il s'assit vis-à-vis d'elle, avec cette crainte et cette timidité que donnent les *véritables* passions» (p. 75: 18-20). It is also used by both the Prince and Nemours to describe their own feelings to Mme de Clèves. The dying Prince speaks of himself as «un homme qui vous aimoit d'une passion *véritable* et légitime» (p. 177: 17-18). In the renunciation scene, Nemours describes his passion as «la plus *véritable* et la plus violente qui sera jamais» (p. 187: 22-23) (12).

As with *vérité*, the initial occurrences of *véritable* set an ironic tone. In its first two uses, it modifies *raisons*: «c'estoit plutost la timidité que donne l'amour que de *véritables* raisons qui causoient les craintes de M. de Clèves» (p. 22: 21-23); Le Cardinal de Lorraine «condamna l'attachement qu'il [le Chevalier de Guise] témoignoit pour Mlle de Chartres avec une chaleur extraordinaire; mais il ne luy en dit pas les *véritables* raisons» (p. 25: 10-12). Here, it is a question of the same inaccessibility of truth as in the discussion of *vérité*, passion, and court intrigue. The narrator's omniscient stance gives the reader the additional information necessary for ironic perception. The vicissitudes of truth, believability, and appearance are reflected in the subsequent occurrences of the adjective, as well as in the incidences of the adverb, *véritablement*.

The story of Sancerre, the first to unite the problems of passion and dissimulation, provides the prototype for later examples of inconstancy. In this episode, *vérité* appears once in association with dissimulation; M. de Clèves describes Mme de Tournon as «une femme qui avoit l'artifice de soutenir, aux yeux du public, un personnage si éloigné de la *vérité*» (p. 62: 30-31). *Véritable* is used twice, its ante- and postposition showing the differing emphasis put on the adjective in each case. Sancerre does not wish to press his marriage to Mme de Tournon «de peur qu'elle ne crûst qu'il le souhaitoit plutôt par intérêt que par une *véritable* passion» (p. 63: 18-19). This is an example of the use of the adjective to certify the authenticity of feeling. In the second case, Sancerre, having learned the truth, complains that he pays «le mesme tribut de douleur que je croyois devoir à une passion *véritable*» (p. 68: 32-33). The postposition, in combination with *croire*, indicates the accrued meaning which the expression «true passion» has acquired for Sancerre (13).

In the novel as a whole, the adverb *véritablement* occurs in the same sense as *véritable* (14). Its three uses in the Sancerre episode illustrate this point. The irony of Sancerre's affirmation to the Prince of Mme de Tournon's genuine grief («Il me répondit qu'elle avoit été *véritablement* affligée,» p. 63: 1) is underlined by M. de Clèves's comment that these explanations did not serve to exculpate Mme de Tournon in his eyes but rather to show him how in love Sancerre was (p. 63: 4-6). The Prince is then also deceived for a time («je crus, aussi bien que lui, qu'elle l'aimoit *véritablement*,» p. 64: 33-34). The retroactive irony here is double. Not only could Sancerre be fooled—as lover he was a notably poor judge—so could M. de Clèves. Finally, as the ultimate and logical result of dissimulation, appearance and reality coincide but are perceived as disparate. The Prince tells his wife, «quand Sancerre crut qu'elle estoit changée pour lui, elle l'estoit *véritablement*» (p. 69: 33-34). Because of the advantage of hindsight, M. de Clèves apprehends the ironies of the inaccessibility of «truth.» The reader, aware of Mme de Clèves's gradually growing passion, has an analogous ironic view of the developing plot, even if he is unaware of the outcome, since his wider knowledge serves partially the same function as hindsight (15).

*Vraisemblable* and *vraisemblance*, by their very nature, underline the problem of the apprehension of «reality» (16). *Vraisemblance* is used for the first time in the Sancerre episode. When Estouteville tells his story, Sancerre first believes his words «parce que j'y ay trouvé de la *vraisemblance*» (p. 67: 27-28), and then, because of his own passion, attempts to discredit this appearance of reality. The same sort of uncertainty often, but not always emotionally induced, may be seen in the other occurrences of *vraisemblance* as well as in the use of the adjective (17).

In the Sancerre episode, as in the whole of *La Princesse de Clèves*, the adjective *vrai* appears only in the locution *il est vrai* (18). Seven of the eighteen uses of the expression are followed immediately by a contradictory *mais* or *néanmoins* (19). All of these statements are in direct discourse, and in each case the character implies that the level of truth perceived by his interlocutor is not profound enough to be accurate. This is made explicit early in the novel (the first instance of this use of the locution) when the Prince reproaches his fiancée with her lack of passion: «*Il est vray* . . . que vous me donnez de certaines apparences dont je serois content s'il y avoit quelque chose au delà; mais, au lieu que la bienséance vous retienne, c'est elle seule qui vous fait faire ce que vous faites» (pp. 31: 33-32: 2; see also Delhez-Sarlet, «Une Page,» pp. 57-58).

On the whole, the expression *il est vrai* is trivialized by its use in ordinary conversation (20). In the case of the narrator, as well as of the characters, certain instances of this locution are more significant than others. The narrator, for example, uses the expression first simply as a transition between two descriptions (21) and again in commenting on Mme de Clèves's love for Nemours: «*Il est vray* aussi que, comme M. de Nemours sentoit pour elle une inclination violente . . . il estoit encore plus aimable qu'il n'avoit acoutumé de l'estre» (p. 38: 1-5). The first usage is insignificant as compared to the second.

There are, however, instances where irony does occur. After warning M. de Clèves that he can tell him nothing upon which to base a sure judgment, the spy begins his account: «*Il est vray* que M. de Nemours a entré deux nuits de suite dans le jardin . . . » (p. 174: 29-30). The irony results from the particular context, but the writer has set up no initial ironic mechanism. The irony which does occur is also a result of the contamination of the more patterned use of other members of the etymological group.

In both occurrences of *il est véritable*, however, irony is present. The expression is used by the narrator to point up Nemours's distorted perception in his immediate reaction to the confession: «*Il estoit véritable* aussi qu'il avoit plusieurs rivaux; mais il s'en imaginoit encore davantage, et son esprit s'égaroit à chercher celuy dont Mme de Clèves vouloit parler» (p. 127: 16-19). The second time the locution appears, the irony seems to be within the character's consciousness (as opposed to being a gloss on it as in the passage just quoted). When, in the renunciation scene, Mme de Clèves first tells Nemours that reasons of duty prevent her from ever marrying anyone, most especially him, Nemours objects that «ce ne sont point de *véritables* raisons» (p. 189: 35). In her response, the Princess opposes her own comprehension of the truth: «*Il n'est que trop véritable* que vous estes cause de la mort de M. de Clèves» (p. 190: 8-9).

In *La Princesse de Clèves*, the characters face the problem of authenticity in a world where word and gesture are capable of shifting, often hidden meanings. For the reader, the controlling artistic framework determines the connotations, and often the denotations of words like *vérité* or *véritable*. Because he stands outside the novel's world, he may perceive the fictional experience ironically. In a carefully wrought context of deception and dissimulation, the reader will lend less credence than usual or, rather, pay more attention than usual to the manner in which these terms are used. The reader of *La Princesse de Clèves* enjoys a truly ironic perspective on the characters' words and deeds.

### 3. *Certitude*

*Certitude* appears only eight times and *certainement* only once. The first two instances of the noun set up an ironic mechanism analogous to the one established by *vérité*. Describing the Prince before he actually proposes, the narrator says, «il eust préféré le bonheur de luy [Mlle de Chartres] plaire à la *certitude* de l'épouser» (p. 30: 5-6). Although the Prince soon discovers that his fear is real, the reader's knowledge outstrips his sufficiently to put this use of *certitude* in an ironic light. Because the information about Mlle de Chartres's feelings is supplied immediately (p. 31: 1-4), the possibilities for the perception of irony involving *certitude*, and not just the general irony of the situation, are increased. When the Prince does propose, the narrator carefully explains how the combination of Mlle de Chartres's gratitude and the Prince's passion allow him to delude himself: «il se flata d'une partie de ce qu'il souhaitoit» (p. 30: 28-29). This is followed by Mlle de Chartres's discussion of the marriage with her mother, where her lack of love is made explicit (pp. 30: 30-31: 4).

*Certitude* is next used in the discussion of astrology. The Queen «soutint qu'après tant de choses qui avoient esté prédites, et que l'on avoit veu arriver, on ne pouvoit douter qu'il n'y eust quelque *certitude* dans cette science» (p. 79: 24-27). Here there are two kinds of irony. If it may be assumed that the seventeenth-century reader was aware of the manner of Henri II's death, the presentation of the prediction in the immediately following context provides retroactive irony. The modern reader, who is more likely to mistrust predictions, might well see the usage of *certitude* as immediately ironic. Unless he was aware of the King's fate, he would probably not perceive any sort of retroactive irony occasioned by the presentation and denigration of the prediction itself. Assuming such a reading, the use of *science* might also contribute to an immediate perception of irony. Although he would be unlikely to remember the specific

words used, the reader would remember the general purport of
the scene. When the King is injured, he is in fact expressly re-
minded of it: «Monsieur le Connétable se souvint, dans ce moment, de la prédiction que l'on avoit faite au Roy, qu'il seroit
tué dans un combat singulier; et il ne douta point que la prédiction ne fust accomplie» (p. 153: 17-20). In this case, there can
be no doubt that the author's use of the historical events is intended to create an ironic situation (see Francillon, p. 126).

The only other use of *certitude* in relation to a secondary
character occurs in the passage on the King's death: «Il receut la
*certitude* de sa mort avec une fermeté extraordinaire» (p. 154:
27-28). While the recurrence of the substantive is undoubtedly
not part of a conscious patterning, its juxtaposition with the use
of *certitude* in the Queen's opinion provides a scaled-down
model of the larger ironic pattern involving *certitude*.

The above uses of *certitude* present, ironically, the problem
of sure knowledge in the realms of sentiment and of events. The
tables are turned in the next occurrence of the noun, where it
conveys the perception of a «real» situation. When the Reine
Dauphine begins to tell the story of the confession, Mme de Clèves's first reaction is to imagine someone else in love with Nemours. As the Dauphine continues to speak, however, the Princess realizes that it is indeed her own story which is being told:
«Si Mme de Clèves avoit eu d'abord de la douleur par la pensée
qu'elle n'avoit aucune part à cette avanture, les dernières paroles de Mme la Dauphine luy donnèrent du désespoir, par la *certitude* de n'y en avoir que trop» (pp. 138: 35-139: 4). In the
heroine's case, certainty, real or supposed, always involves pessi-
mism. Here her despair is caused by her penetration of the partial information given by the Reine Dauphine.

A parallel usage occurs when Nemours's arrival at Coulommiers confirms the heroine's suspicion that she had indeed seen
him in the pavilion: «Cette *certitude* luy donna quelque mouvement de colère» (p. 172: 21-22). Although, by playing on Mme
de Clèves's affections, Nemours succeeds in dissipating some of
her anger, he cannot make her modify her behavior, and she
continues to avoid him (22). The Duke's behavior is, on the one
hand, a proof of the strength of his passion and, on the other,

an example of the sort of indiscretion which makes him no different from other men (see Brody, pp. 113-18, 123-24).

The concept of certainty was first used ironically, and then in the sense of sure comprehension of an unpleasant situation (23). In the renunciation, the uses of *certitude* and *certainement* complete the ironic cycle. Certainty now becomes an experiential absolute by virtue of Mme de Clèves's sentimental education. Obviously, the certainties which she affirms, «la *certitude* de n'estre plus aimée de vous» (p. 191: 32-33) and «puis-je me mettre en estat de voir *certainement* finir cette passion dont je ferois toute ma félicité?» (p. 192: 8-9), are not absolutes from the reader's viewpoint. They are merely high probabilities, an evaluation supported by Nemours's preceding assimilation of this love to his earlier adventures (24). Nonetheless, the reader reacts to the categorical nature of the affirmations, realizing in effect the differentiation between his perception of the heroine's situation and her «real» experience of it. Because so much of the novel serves to convince the reader of the unreliability of judgments, here he remains conditioned to separate himself ever so slightly from Mme de Clèves's affirmations. This minimal doubling of the reader's vision maintains a degree of irony. Thematically, this irony is eliminated by the eventual ending of Nemours's passion. The narrator's evaluative «une passion la plus violente, la plus naturelle et la mieux fondée qui ait jamais esté» (p. 201: 10-12) is juxtaposed with the effects of time on this hyperbolic emotion: «Enfin, des années entières s'estant passées, le temps et l'absence ralentirent sa douleur et éteignirent sa passion» (p. 201: 14-16). In retrospect, it is not Mme de Clèves's *certitude* which is ironic but Nemours's protestations (25).

The discussion of *certitude* dealt with the ironic relationship between the term's denotation and the contexts in which it was used. Although the effects of *certain* are much more diverse, the locution *il est certain*, appearing three times, offers another variation on the theme of knowledge based on the same disparity of literal meaning (26) and situation.

This locution is used to present facts which a speaker deduces from external evidence. In the historical perspective, past events may be considered sure, while their causes often remain veiled.

Two occurrences of *il est certain* deal with just such situations. Mme de Chartres gives two possible motivations for François I's anger at his son's liaison with Mme de Valentinois (p. 41: 22-26). They are followed by the statement «*il est certain* qu'il vid cette passion avec une colère et un chagrin dont il donnoit tous les jours des marques» (p. 41: 26-28). Similarly, in the temporal distancing detailing the consequences of the poor forgery, the narrator, assuming the same retrospective point of view as that imputed to Mme de Chartres in her tale, offers two possible explanations for the way in which the Vidame's fate was sealed (p. 119: 23-28) and follows them with «*il est certain* qu'il ne put jamais se raccommoder sincèrement avec elle [the Queen]» (p. 119: 28-29; *sincèrement* is obviously ironic).

A third instance is found in the Reine Dauphine's description of Nemours's changed behavior: «Mais ce que j'ay le plus d'envie de vous apprendre . . . c'est qu'*il est certain* que M. de Nemours est passionnément amoureux et que ses amis les plus intimes, non seulement ne sont point dans sa confidence, mais qu'ils ne peuvent deviner qui est la personne qu'il aime» (p. 70: 30-35). Here again there is a combination of knowledge and ignorance. As with Mme de Chartres's comment, exterior signs («des marques») betray emotions (27).

Even in retrospect, one can only speculate as to motivation. The past is as unstable a «reality» as the present. This aspect of present reality is exemplified in the courtiers' analysis of Nemours's behavior. His new disinterest in Elizabeth is also a *marque*, and, since love and ambition are men's prime movers (28), the change must certainly be occasioned by love. But all the observation possible *sur place* still leaves one element unexplained (whom he loves), and, thus, knowledge is limited.

Each time *il est certain* is used in such contexts, it represents the speaker's conscious delimitation of his own knowledge. The penetration of appearances is still not sufficient to give full comprehension of a situation, past or present. The reader's relationship to history does not differ from Mme de Chartres's or the narrator's. His relationship to the novel is different, however, as he has long since been told that Nemours is passionately in love with Mme de Clèves (p. 46: 3-7). When the Reine Dauphine enthusiastically tells the Princess of this discovery, the reader is acutely aware not only of the dramatic irony of the situation, focused primarily on Mme de Clèves, but also of the limitations of the Reine Dauphine's deductions. Since the reader knows exactly what is going on, his ensuing sense of superiority makes him perceive the Reine Dauphine's *il est certain* ironically. This irony is focused on the concept of certitude. Thus, in yet another way, Mme de Lafayette underlines a human limitation. In this sense, the novel is, for the reader, a controlled world which makes him aware of this limitation while giving him the illusion that he transcends it.

The ten further occurrences of *certain* touch on the question of knowledge in a different way. What is at stake is the reader's knowledge—in other words, the question of description. In one important example, *certain* conveys the heroine's conviction that Nemours will fall out of love: «La fin de l'amour de ce prince, et les maux de la jalousie qu'elle croyoit infaillibles dans un mariage, luy montroient un malheur *certain* où elle alloit se jeter» (p. 198: 11-14). The phrase «qu'elle croyoit infaillibles» both comments on the meaning of *certain* in postposition, as absolute «certainty,» and illustrates its subjective basis (29).

Exterior signs in the novel are constantly used as keys to hidden emotions (30); as Roxane says, «L'amour le plus discret / Laisse par quelque marque échapper son secret» (*Bajazet*, III, viii, 1119-20). Regretting her behavior during the letter-forging, Mme de Clèves thinks, in like fashion, that «par son aigreur, elle . . . avoit fait paroistre des sentimens de jalousie qui estoient des preuves *certaines* de passion» (p. 120: 16-18). What is interesting about this use of *certain* in postposition is not so much the question of reality or certainty but rather the implied, intrinsic union of love and jealousy. The adjective itself functions to underline this conception.

The functions of *certain* are varied and complex. A simplistic evaluation of them as instances of the author's inability to express herself adequately (e.g. Woshinsky, pp. 46-47) or a holistic assimilation of them to «attenuation» does not adequately account for the information transmitted to the reader (31).

On the whole, the study of the *certitude* set gives results which parallel those of the examination of *vérité*. While the uses of the adjectives and adverbs tend to be more complex, the substantives are part of ironic patterns which allow the reader to trace the convolutions of experience as presented in the novel. Mme de Clèves's *repos*, whether one views it as religious renunciation, secular resignation, illumination and certainty, a desire to preserve her passion, or herself from that passion (32), is clearly a reaction against the instability of «reality» as it is painted in the novel. As the Princess has her *repos*, the reader has irony to give form to the assertion of the chaos of life. It is the patterned use of the two abstract substantives which creates this situation.

*Chapter II*

ATTENUATION AND DESCRIPTION

1. Introduction

Discussions of style in *La Princesse de Clèves* often refer to attenuation, abstraction, and the absence of what the modern reader has come to call «realism.» These qualities are usually treated as ramifications of the social structure described in the novel, assumed to be the same as that in which the author lived. A simplistic assimilation of author to narrator or heroine (e.g. Burkart, p. 160) is scarcely less productive than the more complex, but fundamentally invalid, assumption that the author's struggle to write the novel parallels the Princess' struggle (Niderst, pp. 158-60). While a historical comprehension obviously enriches our understanding of many of the assumptions and value judgments made in the novel, and while a number of the speech patterns (*ne pas haïr*, to give a classic example) have their origins in this historical period, such commentary, when used to explain origins (Woshinsky, pp. 12-13), often does not deal with the esthetic effects resulting from these judgmental and lexical choices.

Jean Fabre sees the form of the novel as the result of a «style de pensée» in which analysis is the predominant mode (*L'Art de l'analyse*, pp. 28, 33, et passim). Others have argued that the reader supplies certain absent details from his own imagination (1). Tiefenbrun, however, has made an important observation in the sense that, rather than seeking to «read into» the understated passages or supply what is «missing,» she seeks to deal with the question within the framework of the text.

My interest in this aspect of the novel was increased by a brief remark made by Gilbert Sigaux in the preface to his edition of the novel (2). He states that «Mme de La Fayette se tient toujours au-dessous de l'intensité vraie des sentiments pour leur donner plus d'éclat et de force dans l'imagination du lecteur. Les *un peu* et les *assez* sont chez elle placés de telle sorte qu'ils chargent les mots qu'ils accompagnent bien plus que ne l'auraient fait des *extrêmement* ou des *très*.»

Because I approach the novel in this study in terms of perspective, the question of description is an essential one. I have therefore chosen a series of terms which are particularly relevant (*quasi, presque, quelque chose, peu, assez, ne . . . guère, quelque* and *chose*) and will use them as a means of inquiry into Mme de Lafayette's famous discretion.

## 2. *Presque* and *quasi*

In her description of Diane's ability to maneuver the King, Mme de Chartres says: «elle fit si bien que le Comte de Taix fut disgracié; on lui ôta sa charge; et, ce qui est *presque* incroyable, elle la fit donner au comte de Brissac» (pp. 44: 22-45: 1). The *presque* represents the avoidance of hyperbole. However, the clause «ce qui est presque incroyable» as a whole serves as an underlining device, delaying the statement of Diane's next move, which the *et* leads the reader to anticipate. Here is an example of the kind of covert emphasis to which Sigaux alludes.

In three cases, *presque* occurs in contexts dealing with the protagonists' emotional or psychological states. The adverb occurs twice in indirect discourse. After forging the letter, Mme de

Clèves reflects on her experience of jealousy: «Elle trouva qu'il estoit *presque* impossible qu'elle pust estre contente de sa [Nemours's] passion» (p. 121: 13-14). The *presque* reflects the element of uncertainty which the character recognizes in her evaluation of the situation. This, then, is not a case of attenuation but, rather, of exact and extremely significant description. The fact is that, until her husband's death, Mme de Clèves lives as though *presque* and not *impossible* were the operative idea. This statement is found near the middle of the novel and reveals the extent to which the heroine still deludes herself. In the heroine's thoughts after her confession, the adverb also serves the end of exact description: «Elle se demandoit pourquoy elle avoit fait une chose si hazardeuse, et elle trouvoit qu'elle s'y estoit engagée sans en avoir *presque* eu le dessein» (p. 129: 12-14). Mme de Clèves had previously thought of confessing to her husband (p. 89: 1-7), but had not consciously planned to do so.

Finally, in the last scene between the Prince and his wife, the narrator says that «M. de Clèves fut *presque* convaincu de son [his wife's] innocence» (p. 179: 5-6). While the adverb does reflect uncertainty, as in the heroine's earlier thought that it was almost impossible she could be satisfied with Nemours's love, it is not used to avoid precise description but, rather, to provide it (3).

A survey of the twenty instances of the synonymous *quasi* (Dubois, Furetière, *Académie*, s.v. «quasi») gives strikingly similar results (4). In seventeen cases, the adverb serves a non-ironic descriptive function, often illustrating the uncertainty born of emotion. For example, in describing Nemours as he observes the confession, the narrator says: «Il estoit si transporté qu'il ne sçavoit *quasi* ce qu'il voyoit» (p. 127: 25-26) (5). There are two uses of *quasi*, both of minor importance, which do seem to reflect the courtly taste for attenuation: the King's comment, «M. de Guise s'offença *quasi* de cette prédiction» (p. 80: 11-12), and the narrator's description of the King at the tourney, «mais le Roy, *quasi* en colère, luy [Montgomery] fit dire qu'il le vouloit absolument» (p. 152: 27-28).

One instance of *quasi*, however, differs from all the others and from all the uses of *presque* as well. When Nemours visits

Mme de Clèves on her return to the court following her mother's death, the Princess is of two minds as to how to react to his veiled declarations. The passage (pp. 76: 31-77: 14) may be divided into three sections. In the first, Mme de Clèves's confusion is shown (e.g. «Elle croyoit devoir parler et croyoit ne devoir rien dire,» pp. 76: 35-77: 1). The middle section contains *quasi*: «Le discours de M. de Nemours lui plaisoit et l'offensoit *quasi* également; elle y voyoit la confirmation de tout ce que luy avoit fait penser Mme la Dauphine; elle y trouvoit quelque chose de galant et de respectueux, mais aussi quelque chose de hardi et de trop intelligible» (p. 77: 1-6). The final section (p. 77: 6-14) contains an explanation of why Mme de Clèves does in fact say nothing: «L'inclination qu'elle avoit pour ce prince luy donnoit un trouble dont elle n'estoit pas maîtresse» (p. 77: 6-8).

The narrator uses the adverb *quasi* to imply, rather than state flatly, that Mme de Clèves is more pleased than offended (6). The narrator feigns limited knowledge for several reasons. To simply state that although the Princess was offended by Nemours's words her pleasure was greater would present the reader with a picture of Mme de Clèves's passion which, while not inaccurate, would no longer possess an analogy to her supposed state of knowledge at this point in the novel. On the one hand, the lack of such an analogy would distort the shared perspective. On the other, the use of *quasi* also provides the reader with ironic insight since the adverb undermines the meaning of *également* and semantically disrupts the series of balanced antitheses used to describe the Princess' state up to this point.

If in this instance *quasi* does translate indefinition (clarified by the subsequent context), the indefinition does not give the reader an impression of vagueness or attenuation but, rather, of subdued irony. It is only in the two cases quoted above (pp. 80: 11-12; 152: 27-28) that the adverb *quasi* truly serves the ends of courtly attenuation.

### 3. *Quelque chose*

*Quelque chose* may be used as a substitute for a more precise
term, as a token for a non-existent word, or simply to designate
a non-specific object (7). In only a few instances is *quelque chose* used in lieu of a more precise term (8). There are ten instances in which an argument can reasonably be made for identifying this usage. Of these, six are found in characters' direct discourse. The expression is used three times by Mme de Clèves, always in conversation with Nemours, twice with the evident motivation of dissimulation, and once out of a desire to spare her
own sensibilities. In his efforts to bring the conversation around
to his passion, Nemours says that the Reine Dauphine has noted
the radical change in his conduct. Mme de Clèves, who has but
recently heard a very full description of this change from the
Reine Dauphine, answers: «Il est vray . . . qu'elle l'a remarqué,
et je crois luy en avoir ouy dire *quelque chose*» (p. 76: 5-6).
Similarly, in a later scene when Nemours asks if the Reine Dauphine has mentioned a lost love letter, the Princess responds:
«Elle m'en a dit *quelque chose*» (p. 113: 10). Since the reader is
aware of what the heroine has actually heard, his perception
of these two statements is ironic. Finally, in the renunciation
scene, to avoid pointedly naming her own feelings, Mme de Clèves asks: «Comment avez-vous pu découvrir . . . que j'aye avoué
*quelque chose* à M. de Clèves?» (p. 188: 14-16) (9). In this case,
the focus of the reader's ironic perception is not on the particular lexical item but on the heroine's question as a whole.

The Vidame, courtier par excellence, uses *quelque chose* in
understatement. Alluding to the possible consequences of the
Queen's discovery that the lost letter belongs to him, the Vidame tells Nemours: «d'un autre côté, je m'attire une haine impla-
cable, qui me coûtera ma fortune et peut-être *quelque chose* de
plus» (p. 100: 33-35). In this instance, the circumlocution
underlined by Nemours's request for an explanation creates curiosity on the part of the reader, who is put in the same position
of ignorance as Nemours.

The same sort of attenuation, although to a lesser degree, appears in the Reine Dauphine's speech. At the ball, she says to

Mme de Clèves: «il y a mesme *quelque chose* d'obligeant pour M. de Nemours à ne vouloir pas avouer que vous le connoissez sans l'avoir jamais veu» (p. 36: 30-32); and in describing Anne Boleyn: «J'ay ouÿ dire que son visage avoit *quelque chose* de vif et de singulier» (p. 83: 2-3). One also finds an example of substitution for a more precise term when the Reine Dauphine tells Mme de Clèves: «Elle [the Queen] croira, et avec apparence, que cette lettre me regarde et qu'il y a *quelque chose* entre le Vidame et moy» (p. 117: 11-13) (10).

*Quelque chose* is also used once to illustrate M. de Clèves's discretion when he reproaches his fiancée for her lack of passion: «Il est vray . . . que vous me donnez de certaines apparences dont je serois content s'il y avoit *quelque chose* au delà» (p. 31: 33-35). This lack of passion is alluded to with equal delicacy by the narrator when she says that, even after the wedding, M. de Clèves «ne laissa pas d'estre son [his wife's] amant, parce qu'il avoit toujours *quelque chose* à souhaiter au delà de sa possession» (p. 33: 25-27). On one level, the locutions parallel each other. The narrator's presentation of the Prince's continued unsatisfaction reveals specific attitudes towards the problem, while in the character's case the locution functions as part of a speech pattern at odds with the intensity of the reproaches made in the scene as a whole (11). It is misleading, also, to assimilate locutions used in the characters' direct speech to those used in the narration, since the reader does not have the same initial attitude toward them and, therefore, cannot possibly perceive them in exactly the same way. The narration, as long as it remains within the conventions of good faith, has greater authority, although it may be read with less interest than the direct discourse. The narrator always handles the question of the Princess' lack of passion for her husband with extreme discretion and, indeed, overtly explains and excuses it (12). For the narrator to have done otherwise would be to invite a simple diagnosis of frigidity, obviating the conflicts around which the novel is centered.

In the passage dealing with Nemours's decision to discuss the lost letter with Mme de Clèves and not the Reine Dauphine as he promised the Vidame, the narrator rephrases Nemours's thoughts, producing an ironic effect. The narrator says: «néant-moins son dessein n'estoit pas de voir la Reine Dauphine et il trouvoit qu'il avoit *quelque chose* de plus pressé à faire» (p. 112: 6-8). This passage is followed by Nemours's speculations on what the Reine Dauphine may have told the Princess, leading to his action («Il alla chez elle . . . ,» p. 112: 13). The slight delay before the explicit statement of what exactly *quelque chose de plus pressé* was is ironic because the reader already knows what Nemours wants to do but must read through the intervening description of his thoughts. The phrasing, «il trouvoit qu'il avoit,» implies a reasoned judgment and contrasts with the subsequent material, creating retroactive irony within the immediate context.

There are four more instances of *quelque chose de* in direct discourse and one more use of the expression by the narrator. These uses differ from the passage discussed above in that none of them represents substitution of a more general for a more specific term (i.e. the use of *amour, passion* or *inclination* instead of *quelque chose au delà*). In two cases, this attenuation may be seen both as reflective of court speech patterns and as an underlining mechanism in the presentation of Mme de Clè-ves's first encounter with Nemours. While the couple dances, the focus is shifted from the description of Nemours's reaction to that of the other observers, avoiding any insight into the Princess' thoughts. The King and Queen «trouvèrent *quelque chose* de singulier de les voir danser ensemble sans se connoître» (p. 36: 12-13). This is followed by the Reine Dauphine's remark in direct discourse (p. 36: 30-32, quoted above), and then by the Chevalier de Guise's remark in indirect form: «il ne put s'empescher de lui [Mme de Clèves] dire que M. de Nemours es-toit bien heureux de commencer à estre connu d'elle par une avanture qui avoit *quelque chose* de galant et d'extraordinaire» (p. 37: 10-14). Each use of *quelque chose de* conveys an impor-tant aspect of the encounter. Each is directly attributed to a character or characters, not to the narrator. Yet each refusal to make a flat statement, from the reader's point of view, stands out as much, if not more, as would absolute judgments. Even on a first reading, the reader is conscious of the fact that this is the encounter for which he has, in effect, been waiting (13). The three uses of *quelque chose de* (one in direct, two in indirect discourse) are combined with the justifying *il était difficile* (14), the use of other characters' reactions to give the central passage a certain indirection, and the narrator's elliptical description of the Princess' conversation with her mother (15). Thus, Mme de Lafayette implies, with no margin for doubt, the import of what has happened. A series of direct hyperbolic statements made explicitly by the narrator would place the encounter on the same plane as the hyperbolic introductory material. Yet it is here that the reader might expect hyperbole, and the attenuations may thus be considered underlining mechanisms. The first five instances of *quelque chose* (16) all relate to the presentation of the central *nœud* and contrast with the hyperbole of the introduction.

In the third usage of *quelque chose de*, it is the indefinition of the expression which is brought out by the context, specifically in the balanced series of antitheses of which this description of the heroine's mixed feelings is a part: «elle y [in Nemours's words] trouvoit *quelque chose* de galant et de respectueux, mais aussi *quelque chose* de hardi et de trop intelligible» (p. 77: 4-6). Here is a case, not of attenuation, or avoidance, but rather of adequately mimetic description. The same may be said of the remaining two occurrences of *quelque chose de*.

In the first case, the aim is to present a pervasive attitude which manifests itself, so to speak, in everything and nothing. This atmosphere is conveyed to the reader by the statement «Il [M. de Clèves] conservoit avec elle le mesme procédé qu'il avoit toujours eu, hors que, quand ils estoient seuls, il y avoit *quelque chose* d'un peu plus froid et de moins libre» (p. 154: 15-18), where not only the locution *quelque chose de* but also the change of subject from the personal *il* to the impersonal *il y avoit* contribute to the indirection of the narrator's description. Combined with the attenuating *un peu*, it also conveys the nonspecific nature of M. de Clèves's attitude.

Secondly, when Mme de Clèves arrives at her dying husband's bedside, Mme de Lafayette writes: «elle luy trouva *quelque chose* de si froid et de si glacé pour elle qu'elle en fut extrêmement surprise et affligée» (p. 175: 13-15). The reader's essential perception of the statement is ironic because he knows the cause of the Prince's state. However, the use of *quelque chose* provides a balancing note of complicity. Had the description read *elle le trouva si froid et si glacé pour elle,* the translation of the heroine's effort to identify exactly her husband's attitude would have been lost. *Quelque chose* provides the note of uncertainty and allows the reader to share some of Mme de Clèves's interiority as well as to continue viewing the scene ironically.

The use of *quelque chose* as a means of avoidance lies almost entirely within the province of the characters' direct discourse, and its use there appears to be motivated by the well-known mixture of emotion and social constraint (for a Spitzerian development of this point, see Burkart, esp. pp. 151-64).

The locution occurs seven more times in direct discourse, either in its own right (i.e. as the only reasonable lexical choice) or as a token for a more complex statement to be made in the immediately succeeding context. Nemours's remark to the Reine Dauphine exemplifies the first usage: «Je croi . . . que je puis penser, sans témérité, . . . que vous aviez dessein de me demander *quelque chose* et que Mme de Clèves s'y oppose» (p. 140: 3-6). The second usage is typified by Mme de Chartres's statement, «si *quelque chose* estoit capable de troubler le bonheur que j'espère en sortant de ce monde, ce seroit de vous voir tomber comme les autres femmes» (p. 56: 21-24) (17).

*Quelque chose* is rarely used as a circumlocution; it appears often in direct discourse, and while understatement is undeniably endemic to the characters' world its use in the narrative is much less pervasive than critics often maintain. One cannot assume that narration and direct discourse are perceived on the same level. One of the particular qualities of *La Princesse de Clèves* is the fact that the language of narration seems indistinguishable from the direct discourse, while in reality the differing levels on which the two are perceived often make virtually the same statement work to different ends.

## 4. *Peu*

The first occurrences of *peu* in the introductory description of the court provide examples of a number of the figures in which this word is used. M. de Clèves's father is described as being «dans un âge un *peu* avancé» (p. 9: 14-15), which is an example of attenuation. An opposite effect is achieved in the description of Nevers's anger at his son's attachment to Mlle de Chartres: «il s'emporta et cacha si *peu* son emportement que le sujet s'en répandit bientost à la cour» (p. 25: 30-32). Formally, this is the opposite of saying «Il s'emporta et fit tellement voir son emportement . . . » Within the context of the court, the natural assumption would be that M. de Nevers would hide his rage from the public. Here, *si peu* functions as litotes and serves to intensify rather than attenuate. The same effect may be seen in two variants of the expression *ne pas etre maître de* (cf. Kaps, p. 12; Tiefenbrun, «The Art,» pp. 49-50): «il [Guise] y fut *si peu* maître de sa tristesse» (p. 33: 18) and «dans un temps où elle [Mme de Clèves] estoit *si peu* maîtresse de ses sentimens» (p. 57: 16-17) (18).

The narrator twice uses *peu* in litotes to describe the heroine. When she sees Nemours stealing her portrait, the narrator says of her: «Mme de Clèves n'estoit pas *peu* embarrassée» (p. 87: 17). This is the first statement of an interiority passage, where the heroine's conflicting thoughts on the proper course of action are presented. The negative form, while not deviating from familiar usage, does command a different sort of attention than would an hyperbole. Here the reader stands outside the character. Initial exclamations by the narrator have the paradoxical effect of both translating the character's agitation and retaining a certain distance. In this passage, however, the concision and brevity of the narrator's resumé of the heroine's thoughts achieve a less emotional tone (p. 87: 17-25).

In the scene in which Nemours visits Coulommiers with his sister, Mme de Clèves accompanies her part of the way in order to avoid remaining alone with Nemours. The narrator comments: «La crainte que cette visite ne fust encore une confirmation des soupçons qu'avoit son mari ne contribua pas *peu* à la

[Mme de Clèves] déterminer» (p. 173: 30-33). The description of the visit contains no extended passages of interiority and no secondary mimesis. The narrator remains at a distance in order to shift attention from one character to another and thus depict the maneuvering in which Nemours and the Princess engage. The use of the litotes here, as in the previous case, both exteriorizes and intensifies, although here the substantivation of the emotion (i.e. «La crainte» instead of *Elle craignait*) increases the degree of distance.

In the description of Nemours, one reads: «Il n'y avoit *aucune* dame dans la cour dont la gloire n'eust été flattée de le voir attaché à elle; *peu de* celles à qui il s'estoit attaché, se pouvoit vanter de luy avoir résisté, et mesme *plusieurs* à qui il n'avoit point témoigné de passion, n'avoient pas laissé d'en avoir pour luy» (p. 11: 4-9) (19). The use of three expressions of quantity in close connection, calling attention to the distinctions being made, illustrates the actualization of *peu de* by specific context.

The heroine echoes this passage in the renunciation scene: «Par vanité ou par goust, *toutes* les femmes souhaittent de vous attacher. Il y en a *peu* à qui vous ne plaisiez; mon expérience me feroit croire qu'il n'y en a *point* à qui vous ne puissiez plaire» (p. 193: 7-10). The first sentence here duplicates the idea in the first clause of the narrator's description. The second clause of each passage also puts forth essentially the same idea, although the narrator, laying the foundation for the Princess' passion and for the favorable evaluation of her resistance, emphasizes Nemours's attractiveness. In the final clause of the Princess' statement, this information is used to justify her passion, emphasize her defensive pride in resisting it, and prepare her for a life of solitude rather than jealousy. Her pride is to some extent a fulfillment of the prophecy implied in the earlier choice of the verb *vanter*. The narrator's third observation is enveloped in the heroine's second. The ordering of these two passages results in two different statements: the narrator's, presenting Nemours as an interesting and almost irresistible figure, and the heroine's, illustrating her final choice.

Actualization by context may also be observed in the description of Mme de Clèves's reaction to Nemours: «il fit, en *peu* de temps, une *grande* impression dans son cœur» (p. 37: 30-31). *Grande* is put into relief through its contrast with *peu*. This studied antithesis is not out of harmony with the rather *précieux* tone in which Nemours is described, especially in the beginning of the novel.

There are many other instances where *peu*, although not actualized in these ways, functions in essentially the same manner—neither to exaggerate nor to understate, but simply to describe (e.g. «Il fit entendre en *peu* de mots,» p. 112: 29-30). In M. de Clèves's reproach to his wife, «vous vous estes repentie mesme du *peu* que vous m'avez avoué et vous n'avez pas eu la force de continuer» (p. 161: 25-27), a judgment is conveyed by the choice of *peu* in favor of *ce que*, for example. These usages parallel the use of *presque* in adequate description.

Three instances of *peu* in direct discourse involve attenuation. Two of these are found in the conversation between Nemours and the Vidame about the lost letter and illustrate court etiquette. Nemours views as «un *peu* extraordinaire» the Vidame's request that he accept authorship of the letter, adding the circumlocutory explanation, «mon intérest particulier m'y peut faire trouver des difficultez» (p. 110: 17-19). The reader, aware of the nature of Nemours's «intérest particulier» and also of the fact that the Princess has the letter, perceives Nemours's maneuvering ironically. Likewise, when the Vidame tells Nemours of «le *peu* de jalousie que je vous vois de M. d'Anville» (p. 111: 19-20), the comment is ironic for the reader possesses more extensive knowledge. Similarly, the reader is conscious of the subversive intent of Mme de Chartres's discreet advice to her daughter: «Je suis d'avis, si ce bruit continue, que vous alliez un *peu* moins chez Mme la Dauphine, afin de ne vous pas trouver mêlée dans des advantures de galanterie» (p. 52: 29-31). The same sort of understatement is found in the indirect description of Mme de Chartres's education of her daughter: «elle luy contoit le *peu* de sincérité des hommes . . . » (p. 17: 21-22). Here an ostensible attenuation assumes an intensifying effect through the subsequent recital of men's infidelities (pp. 17: 22-18: 2). Often attenuation is turned into emphasis by the use of *si* (20). For example, Mme de Clèves pleads with her husband: «trouvez bon que je ne vous parle plus d'une chose [her confessed love for another] qui me fait paroistre si *peu* digne de vous et que je trouve si indigne de moy» (p. 132: 19-21) (21). This is one of several instances in which *peu* plus adjective is used to achieve an effect of emphatic repetition through virtual synonymy. In discussing astrology the King says that he has been told many «choses fausses et si *peu* vraysemblables» (p. 79: 32-33). Likewise, in Nemours's regrets after the repetition of the *aveu* story at the Reine Dauphine's, one reads: «Il estoit inconsolable de luy avoir dit [à Mme de Clèves] des choses . . . qui, bien que galantes par elles-mesmes, lui paroissoient, dans ce moment, grossières et *peu* polies» (p. 148: 15-18).

There are a number of instances where *peu* is used exclusively to suggest the courtly ambiance (22). While some of the narrator's uses of *peu* to describe the protagonists blend in with the courtly motif, they do have more significance, since they help determine the reader's perspective on the main characters. When Mme de Clèves is introduced to Nemours, she «paroissoit un *peu* embarassée» (p. 36: 26-27). The attenuation contributes to the initial convention of presenting the heroine from the exterior.

*Peu* in elliptical description serves a different end in the highly emotional scene between the Prince and his wife following M. de Clèves's attempt to trick her into admitting that the man she loves is Nemours. M. de Clèves's suffering, at least in its nonverbal manifestations, is reduced to the notations that he «s'attendrit» (p. 136: 1) and that he had difficulty speaking. Mme de Clèves «fondant en larmes . . . l'embrassa avec une tendresse et une douleur qui le mit dans un estat *peu* différent du sien» (p. 136: 3-5) (23). Because the Prince is potentially a very sympathetic figure, the description of him is elliptical in comparison to that of his wife, to whom the expression *fondre en larmes*, constituting one of the most physical gestures in the novel, is applied.

In the renunciation scene, the attenuating *peu* occurs in the description of Mme de Clèves. Near the beginning, she looks at Nemours's display of emotion with «des yeux un *peu* grossis par les larmes» (p. 194: 26-27). It is as though Mme de Clèves were seen through Nemours's eyes. The renunciation is more touching because of the presentation of the heroine in as attractive a light as possible (24).

*Peu* occurs once in connection with *quasi* to illustrate the uncertainty caused by extreme emotion. In the description of Nemours observing the confession, one reads: «Il ne sçavoit *quasi* si ce qu'il avoit entendu n'estoit point un songe, tant il y trouvoit *peu* de vraysemblance» (p. 133: 21-23). The adverbial *peu* is used in much the same way, this time in connection with *presque*, to describe Mme de Clèves's reflexions on her experience of jealousy: «Elle fust estonnée de n'avoir point encore pensé combien il estoit *peu* vraysemblable qu'un homme comme M. de Nemours . . . fust capable d'un attachement sincère et durable. Elle trouva qu'il estoit presque impossible qu'elle pust estre contente de sa passion» (p. 121: 8-14) (25).

The occurrences of *peu* fall into three categories: adequate description, ironic understatement, and actualization by context. The second of these is the most interesting since it functions to a variety of ends, on the one hand confirming the traditional notions of court etiquette and, on the other, illustrating, on a smaller scale, many of the foregoing observations on the manipulation of perspective.

### 5. *Ne . . . guère*

Of the seventeen occurrences of *ne . . . guère*, nine are found in direct discourse while eight are part of the narration or passages of interiority. The instances in direct discourse all reflect the courtly penchant for understatement (26). Of these nine occurrences, two are in Mme de Chartres's story, two in the King's remarks on astrology, and one in the Vidame's account to Nemours (27). These five do not differ in usage from the Prince's remark to his wife, «Le repos . . . *n*'est *guère* propre pour une personne de votre âge» (p. 124: 5-6), or the silk merchant's description of Nemours, «il *n*'a *guères* la mine d'estre réduit à gagner sa vie» (p. 182: 18).

This understatement becomes a means of dissimulation in the

Reine Dauphine's account of the *aveu*. Before Nemours's entrance, the Princess had attempted to elicit information, saying, «Cette histoire *ne* me paroist *guère* vraisemblable . . . et je voudrois bien sçavoir qui vous l'a contée» (p. 139: 9-11). For the reader, this statement is ironic. *Ne . . . guère* by its very indefinition (as compared to *ne . . . pas*) serves to underline the deviousness. Two of Mme de Clèves's uses of *quelque chose* illustrate a similar ploy (pp. 76: 5-6; 113: 10). After Nemours arrives, the Reine Dauphine tells him of Mme de Clèves's opinion: «Il *ne* s'en faut *guère* . . . que je ne sois de l'avis de Mme de Clèves, qui soutient que cette avanture ne peut estre véritable» (p. 142: 10-13). This restatement makes the Princess' comment more categorical (*ne* instead of *ne . . . guère*) and serves as a subtle reminder of it.

The narrator's first use of *ne . . . guère* occurs in the brief description of the Prince as «digne de soutenir la gloire de son nom; il estoit brave et magnifique, et il avoit une prudence qui *ne* se trouve *guères* avec la jeunesse» (pp. 9: 16-10: 2). The contrast between this character and Nemours, the «chef-d'œuvre de la nature» (p. 10: 10-11), is striking. Although the Prince displays conventional good qualities, and there is none of the sniping criticism found in other portraits, he merits no hyperbole. The moral note is introduced by «il avoit une prudence qui *ne* se trouve *guères* avec la jeunesse» (p. 10: 1-2). This characteristic sets up a later irony, since his behavior will become imprudent.

The locution *guère moins* occurs twice in the narrative. In the description of Nemours during the confession scene (p. 127: 12-28), the narrator summarizes the Duke's thoughts, but without secondary mimesis, presumably to underline for the reader Nemours's doubts as to whether he *is* the man of whom Mme de Clèves speaks. Near the beginning of the passage, the narrator says of Nemours: «ce que venoit de dire Mme de Clèves *ne* lui donnoit *guère moins* de jalousie qu'à son mari» (p. 127: 13-14). This comparison, which only an outside observer is capable of making, serves as one indication of the distance to be maintained (28).

The other use of *guère moins* produces a similar effect. Near the end of a passage of secondary mimesis, the narrator, as is her habit, initiates a distancing sequence (see Part I, Chapter II). The heroine reflects on her dying husband's fear lest she marry Nemours: «son austère vertu estoit si blessée de cette imagination qu'elle *ne* trouvoit *guère moins* de crime à épouser M. de Nemours qu'elle n'en avoit trouvé à l'aimer pendant la vie de son mary» (p. 184: 21-24). The comparison represents the intervention of a less involved intellect. The litotes calls the reader's attention to the distinction between Mme de Clèves's views of the two actions. The less categorical condemnation of the idea of marrying Nemours helps lay the foundation for her later statement that it is the combination of her sense of duty to her husband and her fear of jealousy which has occasioned her decision and which will sustain her in it (p. 194: 5-10).

In other passages, irony not only affects the reader's perception but defines the narrator's attitude as well. Use of *ne . . . guère* twice serves this end. The description of the Princess' reaction to the lost letter uses both secondary mimesis and exclamations and interventions to express the narrator's sympathy (pp. 96: 28-98: 15). The last paragraph, which prepares the transition to the story of the Vidame de Chartres, begins thus: «Elle *ne* pensa *guères* à l'ordre que Mme la Dauphine luy avoit donné de se trouver à son coucher» (p. 98: 8-9). The foregoing context (pp. 96: 28-98: 7) gives the reader no indication that the Princess gave any thought at all to the order. Therefore, the reader perceives the narrator's comment as ironic (29). This perception changes the reader's perspective, breaking his intense involvement with the heroine and opening the way for the Vidame's story. A similar exploitation of the ironic distancing effect is found in the narrator's comment that the letter was so badly forged «qu'il eust fallu que la Reine *n'*eust *guère* pris de soin d'éclaircir la vérité pour ne la pas connoistre» (p. 119: 12-14).

The uses of *ne . . . guère* illustrate how the same locution can work to different ends, depending on whether it is used by the narrator or in the characters' direct discourse.

## 6. *Assez*

*Assez* is used in three basic ways in *La Princesse de Clèves*. It often appears in the form *assez . . . pour*, where the clause begun by *pour* delimits effect or result (30). Most of these instances present no particular stylistic anomalies: e.g. «je [Sancerre] ne puis la trouver *assez* coupable pour consentir à sa mort» (p. 68: 19-20); «Il [Nemours] inventa une cause de son voyage, *assez* vraysemblable pour la [his sister] tromper» (p. 172: 7-8).

In one case, however, this structure combines with other mechanisms to give an idea of the Prince's hesitancy in approaching Mlle de Chartres: «il songea seulement à tâcher de découvrir s'il estoit *assez* heureux pour qu'elle approuvast la pensée qu'il avoit pour elle» (p. 30: 10-12). The concatenation of verbs (cf. Burkart, p. 157) and the elliptical «la pensée . . . » (31) are the other agents creating this effect.

*Assez* also appears without the delimiting or descriptive *pour* clause. With the exception of the Prince's patently ironic interruption of his spy's report, «C'est *assez* . . . c'est *assez* . . . et je n'ay pas besoin d'un plus grand éclaircissement» (p. 174: 33-35), these usages are also of little interest (32). On the one hand, neither the Prince nor the spy knows «enough» since neither is aware of what happened in the garden. On the other, Mme de Clèves's behavior in the pavilion, while proving her determination to resist, is, nonetheless, a confirmation of her passion for Nemours, and, had the Prince known all this, it could scarcely have pained him less than his suspicions that his wife was unfaithful in a more material way (see Francillon, p. 168).

*Assez* can, however, be used in attenuation or reinforcement (see *Académie*, Furetière, Littré, s.v. «assez»). These contradictory usages open the statements under study here to more than one reading. This indetermination itself gives rise to a sense of attenuation in the larger framework of the whole novel.

Eight of these instances give temporal indications (see section 8). The last of these, «sa vie, qui fut *assez* courte, laissa des exemples de vertu inimitables» (p. 201: 21-23), illustrates the way in which the imprecision provided by *assez* can function in distancing.

By classifying the twenty-one uses of *assez* according to speaker, one discovers that only four are found in direct discourse: two in the Prince's account of the Sancerre affair and two in the Vidame's story (33). These uses are relatively rare in contrast to the seventeen found in the narration (34). It would seem that this relative frequency of *assez* can obscure perception of what the critic, who has reread numerous times, might call its «significant» uses. For example, in the narration one finds both «il se fit un *assez* grand bruit vers la porte» (p. 35: 25-26) and «Il se passa un *assez* grand combat en elle-mesme» (p. 199: 27). By examining only these significant instances, however, one can better understand one of the ways in which the narrator conveys certain important items of information about the protagonists to the reader.

In the first case under study (p. 46: 10-12), groundwork is laid for the presentation of Nemours's love for Mme de Clèves as radically different from his previous romantic entanglements. The reader has been told of the Duke's many mistresses, and of the attention given to each, so that «il estoit difficile de deviner celle qu'il aimoit véritablement» (p. 11: 13-14). He also has been informed of Nemours's «inclination violente» (p. 38: 2) for Mme de Clèves. When the description of the Duke's feelings is resumed after Mme de Chartres's story of Diane de Poitiers (35), «passion» (p. 46: 3) is substituted for «inclination» (see Chapter III below). In telling the reader that Nemours no longer has the patience to pay attention to all his former mistresses, the narrator says: «Mme la Dauphine, pour qui il avoit eu des sentimens *assez* passionez, ne put tenir dans son cœur contre Mme de Clèves» (p. 46: 10-12). Not only does the use of the adjective invite comparison with the first words of the passage, «La passion de M. de Nemours pour Mme de Clèves fut d'abord si violente . . . » (p. 46: 3-4), but the whole locution «sentimens *assez* passionez» also conveys the difference in the nature of the feelings involved, as *passions* is an essence, while *sentimens passionez* is not.

The adverb calls attention to a different sort of distinction in the interview between Nemours and the Princess concerning the lost letter. Following the conclusions Nemours draws from Mme de Clèves's initial refusal to see him (p. 112: 23-25), the first part of the conversation is presented with no commentary; in the sixth *réplique*, a descriptive phrase is added: «répondit Mme de Clèves avec un air *assez* sec» (p. 113: 29-30). At the end of the heroine's speech, another passage presenting Nemours's observations is inserted, for which this descriptive phrase is the effective introduction.

Seen as attenuation, *assez* conveys the conflict between Mme de Clèves's attempt to control the visible signs of her annoyance and her inability to do so. For the reader, owing to his awareness that the Princess is betraying herself, the *assez* reinforces the irony of the scene. Because the design of the passage as a whole makes it appear that the reader and Nemours together observe the heroine, the reader's consciousness of the narrator's presence is minimal, and it is, therefore, not logical to speak here also of an ironic relationship between narrator and character. An indication of such a relationship would, in effect, put the narrator on Nemours's side.

The next instance of *assez* illustrates to what extent sides are taken in the novel. In telling the reader how Nemours comes to recount the *aveu* story, the narrator says that «il tomba dans une imprudence *assez* ordinaire, qui est de parler en termes généraux de sentimens particuliers» (p. 130: 19-20). Although the adverb seems, superficially, to attenuate the adjective (36), it actually calls attention to it by interposing itself between the substantive and its modifier. The narrator's evaluation of Nemours's action verges on the contemptuous, if one considers its juxtaposition with the various laudatory evaluations of Mme de Clèves's confession. Thus, the *assez*, which might be assumed partially to excuse Nemours, actually underlines the implicit condemnation of his behavior (37).

Of all the instances of understatement in *La Princesse de Clèves*, none is more striking than the brief «Il se passa un *assez* grand combat en elle-mesme» (p. 199: 27). Time and feeling are telescoped, and all of the reader's accumulated knowledge leads him, in this instance, to see through the narrator's words (38). This mere allusion to the heroine's intense struggle is perhaps a precursor to Flaubert's «silence» in *L'Education sentimentale*

(1869), where the fifth chapter of Part III ends, «et Frédéric, béant, reconnut Sénécal,» and the sixth begins, «Il voyagea» (39).

*Assez* is a priori less limited in denotation than either *peu* or *ne . . . guère* and, consequently, is a highly flexible tool, ideally suited to the sinuous complexities of the narration in *La Princesse de Clèves*. Examination of its use by the narrator reveals some of the most subtle manipulations of the reader's perception in the novel.

## 7. *Quelque*

With the exception of the question of agreement and the matter of the mode required by *quelque . . . que*, the usage of *quelque* in the seventeenth century does not differ from current practice (Dubois, *Académie*, Furetière, Littré, s.v. «quelque»). In all its forms, *quelque* appears one hundred and forty-two times in *La Princesse de Clèves* (40).

The uses of *quelqu'un* (17 times) and *quelque autre* (pronoun, 5 times) (41) offer no particular anomalies, except in two cases. An effect of expressionist presentation is twice obtained through the use of *quelqu'un*. At the ball, Nemours's presence is experienced by the heroine and presented to the reader, first as a sound, and almost simultaneously as a plausible explanation of that sound: «comme de *quelqu'un* qui entroit et à qui on faisoit place» (p. 35: 26-27). Nemours then becomes «celui qui arrivoit» (p. 35: 30), before Mme de Clèves turns and sees him. Nemours's entrance while the Reine Dauphine is telling Mme de Clèves the *aveu* story is handled in the same way, the Duke being first «*quelqu'un*» (p. 139: 21) and then identified by the Reine Dauphine's «Le voilà lui-même» (p. 139: 25). A similar example of expressionist presentation may be found in Flaubert's «Hérodias,» where the spectator's gradual penetration of the obscurity of John the Baptist's dungeon is described: «ceux qui se penchèrent sur le bord aperçurent au fond quelque chose de vague et d'effrayant. Un être humain . . . » (II, 193).

The attenuating function of *quelque* is made particularly

clear by the use of the adjective in the expression *quelque sorte de* (42). The narrator says that the «*quelque sorte de* jalousie» (p. 30: 7-8) which Guise caused the Prince was due more to his rival's merit than to Mlle de Chartres's behavior (p. 30: 7-10). The locution explicitly indicates that the «jealousy» was in reality only a form taken by the Prince's as yet unexpressed dissatisfaction with his fiancée's attitude. Later, when Mme de Clèves is constrained to take part in the ceremonies surrounding the royal marriages, the narrator says that, since Nemours was occupied with M. de Savoie, Mme de Clèves saw him less often than usual: as a result, «elle s'en trouvoit dans *quelque sorte* de repos» (p. 137: 9). The emphasis here is on the superficial nature of this *repos*. Right after this passage, a new paragraph (P1678; III, 136) begins: «Le Vidame de Chartres n'avoit pas oublié la conversation [about the wife's confession] qu'il avoit eue avec M. de Nemours» (p. 137: 10-11). The juxtaposition is ironic. In these two uses of *quelque sorte de*, the locution indicates that the emotion described is but a simulacrum.

The third use of the locution testifies again to the narrator's practice of underplaying evidence of Mme de Clèves's complicity in her passion. At one point the Princess is upset that Guise has detected her love through her reaction to Nemours's accident; she is also pained by the fact that she has betrayed herself to Nemours: «mais cette dernière douleur n'estoit pas si entière et elle estoit meslée de *quelque sorte de* douceur» (p. 94: 4-5). Similarly, the adverbial *en quelque sorte* is employed once, in the letter-forging scene, to contravene the impression of fully voluntary complaisance: «La présence de son mari et les intérests du Vidame de Chartres la rassuroient *en quelque sorte* sur ses scrupules» (p. 118: 22-24) (43).

These uses illustrate the author's awareness that not all motives are lucidly perceived. In an earlier passage, a similar locution is used to express the as yet partially unconscious nature of Mme de Clèves's passion (44). During the discussion of her absence from Saint-André's ball, she is first annoyed that Nemours might suspect the truth (p. 51: 32-35), «mais ensuite elle sentit *quelque* espèce de chagrin que sa mère lui en eust entièrement ôté l'opinion» (pp. 51: 35-52: 2) (45).

Other instances of *quelque* illustrate the problem of perception and dissimulation (46). With three exceptions, these uses,
when grouped by function, are all found either in direct discourse or in obviously identifiable indirect discourse (47). The
three passages which do not conform are, nonetheless, resumés
of thought presented by the narrator, and they parallel instances in which one character describes another's thoughts. For
example, the Prince says: «Sancerre crut voir *quelque* refroidis-
sement dans la passion qu'elle [Mme de Tournon] avoit pour
luy» (p. 63: 28-29). Describing the Queen's reaction to the obviously forged letter, the narrator says: «elle crut que la Reine
Dauphine y avoit sa part et qu'il y avoit *quelqu'*intelligence
entr'eux [the Reine Dauphine and the Vidame] » (p. 119: 18-
19). In these two passages, as in the others in this category
(48), the adjective conveys the mixture of certainty and uncertainty which constantly plagues people at court, and by ex-
tension all those who live in society. This observation is confirmed by the fact that in all but one case, there is a collocation
of these usages with a verb of supposition (*croire, penser, craindre, paraître à quelqu'un, savoir, connaître, juger* and *sembler à
quelqu'un*) (49).

The reader is sometimes placed in an analogous situation concerning the information given in the novel when the narrator
offers two possible explanations of an event. One of the two
possible reasons for Guise's accurate understanding of Mme de
Clèves's reaction to Nemours reads this way: «soit qu'en effet il
eust paru *quelque* trouble sur son [Mme de Clèves's] visage»
(p. 37: 7-8).

Another use of *quelque* occurs in the initial description of
Nemours: «Il avoit tant de douceur et tant de disposition à la
galanterie qu'il ne pouvoit refuser *quelques* soins à celles qui tâchoient de lui plaire» (p. 11: 9-12). Collocated with *tant de*, the
ironic potential is actualized. *Quelque* serves as what might be
called an emphatic partitive. Carrying the supplementary nuance of «not much» or «not many» (50), *quelque* gives a greater degree of definition than the partitive. Here it is used to ironic effect (51).

A weaker kind of irony attends the heroine's certainty that

Nemours was in fact the man whom she had seen in the pavilion: «Cette certitude luy donna *quelque* mouvement de colère, par la hardiesse et l'imprudence qu'elle trouvoit dans ce qu'il avoit entrepris» (p. 172: 21-23). The attenuating adjective, in combination with the analysis of the anger (52), makes it clear to the reader that the heroine's annoyance is centered on Nemours's behavior, not on the Duke himself, and that her passion is really in no way altered by it. The incident, however, reinforces Mme de Clèves's realization that Nemours is not «différent du reste des hommes» (p. 147: 31-32; see Brody, pp. 123-24).

As *quelque sorte de* conveys the superficial or illusory nature of certain feelings, so a number of the adjectival *quelque* tell us that the feeling involved is provisional. When, for example, the narrator describes the Prince's reaction to the letter his wife has written him after their argument over Nemours's abortive visit, one reads: «cette lettre fit de l'impression sur M. de Clèves et luy donna *quelque* calme» (p. 163: 1-2; see also pp. 171: 34; 197: 4-6). It is the use of the adjective in place of the partitive which gives the reader that sense of superior knowledge which founds ironic perception. In another example, Mme de Clèves decides to travel to her lands in the Pyrenees: «Elle jugea que l'absence seule et l'éloignement pouvoit luy donner *quelque* force» (p. 198: 18-20). Here a deepened sense of her own strengths and weaknesses has narrowed the ironic gap between reader and character.

*Quelque* as emphatic partitive can also reflect desperation. When M. de Clèves says to his wife «ayez *quelque* compassion de l'estat où vous m'avez mis» (p. 132: 24), the statement meaning *un peu de* is more forceful than would be *ayez de la compassion* (53). In Sancerre's statement, «je trouvois *quelque* douceur à penser que je ne devois jamais me consoler» (p. 68: 29-30) (54), this nuance is actualized by a semantic contradiction, a sort of large-scale oxymoron (*douceur | ne jamais se consoler*).

The complexities of the narrative are well illustrated in the usage of *quelque*. When one steps back from the text, the frequent use of the adjective gives an impression of imprecision.

Thus, *quelque* helps create a general linguistic ambiance of in-definition (see below, section 9). However, perceived syntag-matically in situation, the various instances of *quelque* produce many different effects, only some of which may be adequately understood by classing them under the rubric of indefinition.

## 8. Temporal Indications

*Peu, quelque, quelquefois* and *assez* are all used to give tem-poral indications in *La Princesse de Clèves*. In her study of time in the novel, Claudette Sarlet concludes that, while in the pas-sages dealing with the protagonists' passions (her example is the letter episode) Mme de Lafayette gives indications of *la durée*, the question of chronology in general is of less importance since the events serve as a background for the development of a pas-sion (55). Although Sarlet does not specifically mention them, the majority of the uses of *peu, quelque, quelquefois*, and *as-sez* in reference to time manifest the author's disinterest in es-tablishing a firm historical chronology (e.g. «*peu* de jours avant les nopces,» p. 32: 19-20; «Mme de Chartres combatit *quelque* temps l'opinion de sa fille,» p. 50: 18-19; cf. Tiefenbrun, p. 79).

By nature indefinite, *quelquefois* may serve the end of cir-cumlocution, as in the Princess' comment in the confession scene: «je veux éviter les périls où se trouvent *quelquefois* les personnes de mon âge» (p. 125: 11-12). Three other uses of the adverb (pp. 182: 15; 182: 24; 196: 7) all apply to Nemours's observation of Mme de Clèves from the silk-merchant's window, placing these events in that indefinite period of time between the Prince's death and the parallel resurgence of the heroine's feelings and Nemours's decision to force an interview.

Two passages might be suggested as supplements to Sarlet's comments on *la durée*. The first contains the remaining two uses of *quelquefois*: «les soins qu'elle [Mme de Clèves] luy [the Prince] rendoit, et son affliction, qui luy paroissoit *quelquefois* véritable et qu'il regardoit aussi *quelquefois* comme des marques de dissimulation et de perfidie, luy causoient des sentimens si opposez et si douloureux . . . » (p. 176: 14-19). The repetition

of the adverb provides a sense of intermittence and vascilla-
tion, thereby giving the reader a sense of the subjective time
perceived by the Prince (cf. Tiefenbrun, p. 30).

The second passage occurs at the beginning of that first difficult interview between Nemours and the heroine after her
mother's death: «Mme de Clèves n'estoit pas moins interdite, de
sorte qu'ils gardèrent *assez longtemps* le silence. *Enfin* M. de Nemours prit la parole et luy fit des compliments sur son affliction; Mme de Clèves, estant bien aise de continuer la conversation sur ce sujet, parla *assez longtemps* de la perte qu'elle avoit
faite; et *enfin*, elle dit que . . . » (p. 75: 21-27). The alternation
and repetition of *assez longtemps* and *enfin* translate the tense
atmosphere (56).

### 9. *Chose*

*Chose* and *passion* are the two most frequently occurring
common nouns in *La Princesse de Clèves* (57). The double nature of the novel is illustrated in this simple statistic. The high
incidence of *chose* (relative to other common nouns) seems to
be one of the major factors in explaining the critics' frequent
assessment of Mme de Lafayette's style as elliptical and abstract. This observation is confirmed by the common reaction
to *La Princesse de Montpensier* and *La Comtesse de Tende*.
Both deal with similar themes and are often assumed to be ver-
sions of *La Princesse de Clèves*. The impression that the style of
this latter novel is the most elliptical, with that of *La Princesse
de Montpensier* resembling it more closely that the style of *La
Comtesse de Tende* (58), is borne out by the relative frequen-
cies of *chose* and *passion* in these two novellas. In *Montpensier,
passion* is the most frequent common noun, appearing only one
more time than *chose*. In *Tende*, on the other hand, *passion* is
fifth among the nouns and appears three times as often as *chose*
(59). Yet here, even more than in the case of *assez* (see above,
section 6), the overall impression created by the frequency of
*chose* may sometimes subsume a rather different reality. The
statistics, revealing at one level, remain incapable of elucidating

the specific ways in which the item is used (see Delhez-Sarlet, «Une Page,» p. 66).

In the *dénouement*, for example, *chose* appears as part of a particular sort of fixed expression (60). Of Mme de Clèves's illness, one reads: «Cette veue si longue et si prochaine de la mort firent [*sic*, P1678, IV, 201] paroistre à Mme de Clèves les *choses* de cette vie de cet œil si différend dont on les void dans la santé» (p. 199: 17-19). The phrase «les *choses* de cette vie» calls up religious associations. The following lines announce the theme of renunciation: «La nécessité de mourir, dont elle se voyoit si proche, l'accoustuma à se détacher de toutes *choses* et la longueur de sa maladie luy en fit une habitude» (p. 199: 20-22). This instance of «toutes choses» contrasts with the earlier use of the expression to describe Mme de Valentinois's power: «Depuis douze ans que ce prince règne, elle est maîtresse absolue de *toutes choses*» (p. 44: 13-14). *Chose* occurs again in Mme de Clèves's message to Nemours: «ayant trouvé que son devoir et son repos s'opposoient au penchant qu'elle avoit d'estre à luy, les autres *choses* du monde luy avoient paru si indifférentes qu'elle y avoit renoncé pour jamais» (p. 200: 29-32). The tone is again quasi-religious (see Sweetser, pp. 490, 491, n. 23; cf. Francillon, pp. 177-79). *Chose* appears here as part of a specialized language.

*Chose* often appears with verbs of speech (61). In most cases, the noun is modified within the sentence itself and its denotation made clear by the preceding or following context (62). In the novel, as in ordinary speech, *chose* is used as an abbreviated referent for whole situations or concepts which, once stated, are not repeated. Referring to the failure of the negotiations for Mlle de Chartres's marriage to the Prince Dauphin, the narrator comments: «L'on peut juger ce que sentit Mme de Chartres par la rupture d'une *chose* qu'elle avoit tant désirée» (p. 27: 29-30). Not only does the preceding context define *chose*, but a few lines above the reader also learns that Mme de Valentinois had been «avertie du dessein de ce mariage» (p. 27: 24-25). The use of *chose* also avoids a more specific sort of repetition of *mariage* or a related term such as *alliance*. There are a large number of instances in which, as here, one could, with little ingenuity, substitute another noun for *chose* (63). It is not that these cases are in themselves unclear but, rather, that their frequency gives the impression that the novel's language is elliptical.

There are, of course, instances in which the use of *chose* is expressly elliptical. It is a good means of dispensing with details. When Nemours loses interest in Elizabeth, «il ne pressa plus avec tant d'ardeur les *choses* qui estoient nécessaires pour son depart» (p. 46: 14-15). It allows the narrator to skip over the unimportant parts of conversations. When Mme de Clèves returns to the court after her mother's death, the Reine Dauphine visits her, but only the descriptions of Nemours are in direct discourse. All the preceding court gossip is dispensed with by the indirect statement that the Reine Dauphine «lui conta en suite plusieurs *choses* particulières» (p. 70: 28-29) (64). The same pattern also occurs in narratives given by the characters, as when, in recounting the Sancerre affair, the Prince tells his wife: «je dis plusieurs *choses* qui firent connoître à Mme de Tournon l'imprudence qu'elle avoit faite» (p. 62: 14-15). In telling his story, the Vidame uses *chose* to dispense with unimportant information (p. 102: 5-6), but, as is typical of this consummate courtier, he also uses the noun to allude to secrets, real or imagined: «je savois beaucoup de *choses* dont je n'avois jamais parlé» (p. 101: 26-27). As might be expected, in direct discourse *chose* becomes an instrument of deliberate vagueness in those frequent situations where directness is either impossible or impolitic (e.g. pp. 79: 8-10; 141: 6-7; 187: 23-24).

Analogous linguistic behavior is found in the letter-forging scene where the narrator uses *chose* to special advantage: «ce prince [Nemours]. . . ne faisoit que l'[Mme de Clèves] interrompre et luy dire des *choses* plaisantes» (p. 118: 33-35). This use of *chose* in lieu of a reproduction of Nemours's pleasantries is one of the techniques Mme de Lafayette exploits in order to present only a schematic picture of the Princess' flirtatious complicity in this scene. Likewise, in telling the reader how Mme de Clèves, despite her best efforts, was unable to hide her feelings from Nemours, the narrator uses a number of justificatory mechanisms (pp. 81: 33-82: 1). But even before these justifications, the narrator describes Mme de Clèves thus: «Quelque application qu'elle eust à éviter ses [Nemours's] regards et à lui parler moins qu'à un autre, il lui échapoit de certaines *choses* qui partoient d'un premier mouvement, et qui faisoient juger à ce prince qu'il ne lui estoit pas indifférent» (p. 81: 29-33). The use of *chose* in place of a more delimited term, such as *marques*, does not give the reader a really precise picture of how Mme de Clèves gave herself away. In combination with the impersonal verbal construction (the heroine as indirect object not subject), this use of *chose* results in the same disculpation of the heroine as the manipulation of the letter-forging or pavilion scenes.

These are situations where the less precise, *chose*, takes the place of the more precise. A different pattern occurs in the Reine Dauphine's comments on her mother: «c'est une *chose* remarquable que, veuve d'un Duc de Longueville, trois rois ayent souhaité de l'épouser» (p. 29: 9-11). The elimination of *chose* through the use of *il est remarquable* would shorten the statement and make it less concrete. There are approximately twenty-two occurrences of the use of *chose* to lend a degree of concreteness to statements which would otherwise be even more abstract (65). In most cases, as in the passage quoted, the use of *chose* does not serve a more specific purpose. However, of the narrator's seven uses of *chose* in this manner (66), four do produce a more particular effect (67). The additional focus provided by *chose*, as opposed to *ce que*, arouses the reader's curiosity: «Elle [Mme de Chartres] fut entièrement confirmée dans les soupçons qu'elle avoit de cette inclination,» the narrator explains, «par une *chose* qui arriva peu de jours après» (p. 47: 5-8). *Une chose* is vaguer than *ce que* would have been and plays down the narrator's omniscience with the result that the reader is made to discover something through the succeding events, thereby sharing Mme de Chartres's perspective. In general, the uses of *chose* to make statements more concrete help create the impression of weightiness in Mme de Lafayette's style (68).

While there are more instances of *chose* which could be explicated, the above examples give an adequate picture of its main uses. It is in essence by virtue of its high frequency, rather than through special effects, that *chose* is a prime factor in the perception of the novel's style as elliptical and, at the same time, somewhat ponderous (69). I am not proposing a defense of Mme de Lafayette's style on the basis of lightness or grace. However, it should be clear from a number of the specific passages of the narrative examined (e.g. the exploitation of *chose*'s vagueness in the letter-forging scene) that abstraction is often a false category. The comparison of portions of the text with more specific terms which could logically be substituted is a useful tool for pinpointing the effects created by the text itself. It is erroneous, however, to consider the text as somehow «lacking» more specificity. Those matters treated elliptically in the narrative shape the reader's perspective as much as do those matters treated in detail.

## 10. Conclusion

The length and complexity of these analyses point out with sufficient force the danger of generalization. There are, however, a number of threads which run through the various sections. In all cases, the lexical item is used in a number of different, often contradictory ways. In many instances, the items appear in natural speech patterns (i.e. where the concept of lexical choice is irrelevant).

Likewise, there are many cases of what I have called adequate description. The particular item is not part of a figure, but simply represents a fact or situation. One of the major problems encountered in critical commentary on Mme de Lafayette's style is the concept of «description» applied to the novel. The absence of physical detail conflicts with the norms generally assumed to apply to the novel, considered, at least until the advent of the anti-novel, the literary genre which was closest to «ordinary speech» and «real life.» A definition of the word *description*, however, contains no restrictions on the object of the process (70). Further, there is a tendency to confuse mimesis (71) with description (72). Even when studying terms purposely selected for their indeterminate or attenuative value, no paucity of «descriptive» usages is to be found.

As for understatement, there is a difference between the ways the reader perceives this figure in the characters' direct discourse and in the narrative. In the former, it is often associated with dissimulation, although it may sometimes be considered merely the product of a certain social norm. In the latter, understatement serves to guide the way in which the reader sees the characters (e.g. the attempt not to show the heroine in too unfavorable a light) or to create irony. The use of understatement creates ironic distance by providing norms within the novel against which certain of the narrator's descriptions of the characters may be measured.

The frequent use of some of the terms studied, especially *quelque* and *chose*, gives the reader an overall impression of attenuation or vagueness. Closer examination reveals that, in situation, these terms often have quite different effects, particularly in relation to the protagonists, on whom the reader's attention is centered.

If one sought to give, in one sentence, the conclusion to be drawn from the lexical surveys in this chapter, one might well quote Jacques Chardonne's description of Mme de Lafayette's style as «à la fois précis et enveloppé» (73).

*Chapter III*


SENTIMENTAL VOCABULARY


The thematic significance of the high frequency of *passion* is self-evident (1). It should be noted, however, that of all the occurrences of the noun, only three may be interpreted in the more general sense of feelings or emotions, while in all other cases the substantive refers to love (2). Used in the wider sense, the noun is plural. Nemours uses *passions* in his conversation with Mme de Clèves after her mother's death. The Princess has just spoken at length of her grief; Nemours replies: «Les grandes afflictions et les *passions* violentes . . . font de grands changemens dans l'esprit; et, pour moy . . . » (pp. 75: 30-76: 1). The Duke here exploits the substantive's potentially extended meaning to bring the conversation around discreetly to his own love. Another instance is found in Mme de Clèves's famous statement, «J'avoue . . . que les *passions* peuvent me conduire; mais elles ne sçauroient m'aveugler» (p. 192: 25-26). Here the generalization subsumes very intentional specificity. However, when the narrator says «Les *passions* et les engagemens du monde luy [Mme de Clèves] parurent tels qu'ils paroissent aux personnes qui ont des veues plus grandes et plus éloignées» (p. 200: 1-4), the phraseology, borrowed from a theological context, makes it clear that *passions* is to be taken in the generalizing sense. But while the meaning of the phrase «Les passions et les engagemens du monde» is not in question, the nature of its real referent produces a special effect. Although the court is not presented as unattractive, nor the Princess' friends there as unpleasant to her, there is no evidence that she feels any particular attachment to them. From the beginning, she is so consumed by her love that no other concern really touches her. The absence of «realist» detail centers the reader's attention on Mme de Clèves's passion. Just as the day-to-day lives of the characters seem blurred to the reader, so the intensity of the heroine's dilemma renders her insensitive to routine daily events (3).

There are six other occurrences of *passion* in the plural, and, although the noun is always used in the sense of love, the choice of the plural sometimes has special thematic or stylistic implications (4). Two instances of the plural do illustrate the difference between Nemours and Mme de Clèves. The noun is sometimes used in the sense of discrete attachments (5), as in this case. Nemours asks himself, «Est-il possible que l'amour m'ait si absolument osté la raison et la hardiesse et qu'il m'ait rendu si différent de ce que j'ay esté dans les autres *passions* de ma vie?» (p. 185: 17-20). The opposition with *amour* clarifies the use of *passions* in the sense of love affairs. Nemours is the only character in connection with whom the expression *les autres passions* is used. This is, of course, one of the two motivating forces in Mme de Clèves's decision; in the renunciation which follows the passage just quoted, she makes this explicit: «Vous avez déjà eu plusieurs *passions*, vous en auriez encore» (p. 192: 30-31).

In general, the distribution of *passion* through the novel follows the pattern of gradual intensification and streamlining of the plot, while the distribution of the substantive in the «digressions» points up their thematic function (6). A clear pattern emerges from the narrator's use of *passion* to describe the heroine's feelings and Mme de Clèves's use of the word in reference to herself (i.e. direct and indirect discourse as well as certain passages of interiority). The first use of *passion* by Mme de Clèves herself is found in an indirect indication of interiority:

«quand elle ne le [Nemours] voyoit plus et qu'elle pensoit que ce charme qu'elle trouvoit dans sa vue estoit le commencement des *passions*, il s'en falloit peu qu'elle ne crûst le haïr par la douleur que luy donnoit cette pensée» (p. 55: 22-26). The force of *des passions* is diminished by its function as the complement of *le commencement*. Mme de Clèves's conscious admission of her love is not yet complete.

The narrator first expressly qualifies Mme de Clèves's feelings as *une passion* when introducing the interiority sequence following the reading of the letter: «Quelle vue et quelle connoissance pour une personne de son humeur, qui avoit une *passion* violente» (p. 96: 32-34). The directness of this passage clarifies the function of jealousy in the novel as both the revealer and the destroyer of love. The contrast between the narrator's flat classification of the Princess' feelings (intensified by *violente*) and the fairly elliptical and ironic way in which they have previously been presented creates for the reader, as does the exclamatory form as a whole, an analogue of the heroine's shock and surprise.

When Mme de Clèves, in her remorse after the forging of the letter, finally admits to herself the full extent of her involvement, *passion* makes its next appearance: «Quand elle pensoit . . . que, par son aigreur, elle luy [Nemours] avoit fait paroistre des sentimens de jalousie qui estoient des preuves certaines de *passion*, elle ne se reconnoissoit plus elle-mesme» (p. 120: 12-18). The revelatory function of jealousy is made explicit here, since her analysis is made as though from Nemours's point of view [i.e. the sign *aigreur* denotes jealousy (7) *ergo* the existence of *passion*], and it is through this involuntary exteriorization that Mme de Clèves comes to terms, in a very literal sense, with the nature of her love.

The substantive appears only twice in Mme de Clèves's direct discourse, once in the renunciation (p. 192: 25-26) and once in soliloquy. After the disclosure of the *aveu*, the heroine's anguish and rage against M. de Nemours are presented in soliloquy. It is not only her disillusionment with Nemours which troubles her (see Brody, pp. 123-24), but also the result of his indiscretion: «Je seray bientost regardée de tout le monde comme une personne qui a une folle et violente *passion*» (pp. 147: 35-148: 1). As in the previous case (p. 120: 12-18), the Princess views her love in the mirror of others' eyes. The adjectives convey this judgment (8).

From this point on, the narrator's handling of *passion* in reference to the heroine changes. The next mention of Mme de Clèves's love is in the matter-of-fact «Mme de Clèves l'aimoit aussi [Mme de Martigues] comme une personne qui avoit une *passion* aussi bien qu'elle» (p. 164: 9-11). This is closely followed by the narrator's equally matter-of-fact «deux jeunes personnes, qui avoient des *passions* violentes dans le cœur» (p. 164: 29-30). The next occurrence describes the heroine in the pavilion, putatively through Nemours's eyes, and illustrates the narrator's free acceptance of the term as proper to describe Mme de Clèves's love: «elle s'assit et se mit à regarder ce portrait avec une attention et une rêverie que la *passion* seule peut donner» (p. 167: 19-21) (9).

However, the more common use of *passion* does not preclude the stronger sense of the word in passages of interiority. After the Prince's death, *passion* is used to associate Mme de Clèves's sense of guilt with her love: «Quand . . . elle considéra qu'elle estoit la cause de sa mort, et que c'estoit par la *passion* qu'elle avoit eue pour un autre qu'elle en estoit cause, l'horreur qu'elle eut pour elle-mesme et pour M. de Nemours ne se peut représenter» (pp. 179: 27-180: 3). The narrator's resumé appears later in the same sequence: «elle se faisoit un crime de n'avoir pas eu de la *passion* pour luy [her husband] » (p. 181: 2-3). This language contrasts sharply with the initial notation that Mlle de Chartres would marry the Prince with less repugnance than another (p. 31: 1-4) and the elliptical «M. de Clèves ne trouva pas que Mlle de Chartres eust changé de sentiment en changeant de nom» (p. 33: 20-21). Distinctions which were once beyond her comprehension (p. 32: 13-14) now strike her with agonizing clarity. While all this is conveyed by the passage (pp. 180: 33-181: 8), it is nonetheless true that it represents, with the subsequent justificatory intervention (p. 181: 3-4), the narrator's summary of the heroine's thoughts. The use of *passion* in collocation with *crime* gives the statement the force which parallels the character's state.

In presenting the heroine's reaction to seeing Nemours in the garden, the narrator again uses *passion* for dramatic effect: «Quelle *passion* endormie se ralluma dans son cœur, et avec quelle violence!» (p. 183: 26-27). The mixed metaphor, criticized by Valincour (p. 267), illustrates the extent to which the standard figures of sentimental language had become assimilated into normal expression, gradually losing their original double (metaphorical) meaning, and, consequently, becoming susceptible to this sort of amalgamation (cf. Niderst, p. 185).

In the narrator's descriptions of Mme de Clèves's love for Nemours, the use of *passion* becomes more frequent with the growing explicitness of the emotion. This progression parallels Mme de Clèves's gradual admission to herself of her feelings. The narrator's use of *passion*, however, is initially a step ahead of Mme de Clèves's conscious admission of her state, giving rise to irony. The noun is almost entirely absent from the heroine's direct discourse, illustrating the restraint which she imposes on the verbal manifestation of her feelings. In the case of Nemours and the Prince, *passion* is applied to their love, as to Guise's, from the outset (pp. 19: 24-25; 25: 25; 46: 3-4), pointing out Mme de Clèves's role as an inspirer of passion. The theme of M. de Clèves's unrequited love for his wife is hammered home eight times in Part I (10) by the use of *passion* in reference to him.

The other terms denoting or connoting love conform to essentially the same pattern. The group *amour, amoureux, aimer*, is, naturally the most prominent. The adjective *amoureux* (appearing approximately fifty-four times) (11) is never used to describe Mme de Clèves; only twice is it applied to the Prince, both times in the first part of the novel (pp. 22: 14; 30: 27). Nemours, on the contrary, is often qualified as *amoureux* by both the narrator and the other characters (e.g. pp. 37: 6; 55: 20; 70: 32; 86: 17). *Amoureux* is first used in the opening presentation of the court: «Ce prince [Henri II] estoit galant, bien fait, et *amoureux*» (p. 5: 3-4). The majority of the occurrences of the adjective are found in the first half of the novel (thirty-seven in Parts I and II, seventeen in III and IV) and, as would also be expected, the distribution of the twenty usages referring directly or indirectly to Nemours traces the outline of his role (Part I, 4; II, 4; III, 8; IV, 4).

*Aimer* is also used frequently (12). As with *passion*, however, the verb does not appear until rather late in the novel to describe Mme de Clèves's love of Nemours: «Elle ne se flatta plus de l'espérance de ne le pas *aimer*» (p. 77: 26-27). Again, as with *passion*, the verb is gradually used more explicitly, both by narrator and character. The final exteriorization takes place in the renunciation: «Ayez cependant le plaisir de vous estre fait *aimer* d'une personne qui *n'auroit* rien *aimé*, si elle ne vous avoit jamais veu» (p. 195: 8-10). Even here the form remains indirect. The purport, however, is the same as a direct declaration, and it is in this light that the heroine sees her behavior: «ce luy estoit une chose si nouvelle d'estre sortie de cette contrainte qu'elle s'estoit imposée, d'avoir souffert, pour la première fois de sa vie, qu'on luy dist qu'on estoit amoureux d'elle, et d'avoir dit elle-mesme qu'elle aimoit» (p. 196: 14-18). The use of *on* adds more generality to the hyperbole, thus conveying to the reader the way in which Mme de Clèves's passion so fills her momentarily that it is as if her husband had never existed.

The use of *vérité* and *certitude* showed that the theme of emotionally distorted perception was, for Mme de Lafayette, a major novelistic principle. Much of the force of M. de Clèves's «Je vous *aimois* jusqu'à estre bien aise d'estre trompé» (p. 176: 30-31) comes from his conscious, explicit statement of this theme which underlies the picture of passion painted in the novel.

The noun *amour* is used only half as often as *passion* (13). The frequency of the noun increases quite regularly as the novel unfolds (Part I, 8; II, 9; III, 10; IV, 14). It first occurs in the most generalized sense in the narrator's statement «elle [Mme de Chartres] faisoit souvent à sa fille des peintures de l'*Amour*» (p. 17: 18-19). The use of upper case here (P1678, I, 38) and in «l'*Amour* estoit toujours meslé aux affaires et les affaires à l'*Amour*» (p. 23: 22-23; P1678, I, 60) may be indicative of Mme de Lafayette's intentional use of *amour* as a personified force, although, without a manuscript, it is impossible to be certain of this.

Mme de Clèves also uses *amour* in the generalized sense: «Et veux-je enfin m'exposer aux cruels repentirs et aux mortelles douleurs que donne l'*amour*?» (p. 121: 18-20). Here, in her reaction to the letter incident, the conception of love which the heroine has come to accept is defined. She will never again be able to see in love only «ce qu'il a d'agréable» (p. 17: 20), although she remains sensitive to the «charmes de l'amour» (p. 197: 4).

When modified by a possessive adjective, *amour* is used almost exclusively in reference to Nemours. It is difficult to determine the exact difference in connotation between *amour* and *passion* since contemporary dictionaries define each in terms of the other (Furetière, s.v. «amour,» «passion»; *Académie*, s.v. «aimer,» «pâtir»). The greater frequency of *passion*, however, considered in relation to the presentation of love as overpowering and destructive, would tend to indicate that *passion* has more negative connotations than *amour*. It is, therefore, logical that while Mme de Clèves's love for Nemours comes to be described as *passion*, the use of *amour* is much more prevalent in referring to his love for her. The use of *amour* to describe Nemours's love reminds the reader of his (at least temporary) sincerity. Because in the latter portions of the novel *passion* is used both by the narrator and Mme de Clèves to qualify her love, the disapproval which the heroine feels for her love is conveyed to the reader.

The heroine's gradual admission and comprehension of this love is conveyed through the use of *inclination*. Because the word implies a natural disposition, it absolves one of responsibility for the disposition itself, although not for the handling of it (14). For modern man, such naturalness is often a positive value. A glance at *La Carte de Tendre*, however, shows the light in which *inclination* was seen in the seventeenth century. The river leads directly to «Tendre sur Inclination» and beyond into «La Mer dangereuse.» After Mme de Clèves first sees Nemours, her potential passion is presented through the eyes of other characters (Guise and Mme de Chartres, p. 37), and then through a series of comments by the narrator. First the reader is told that Nemours made «une grande impression dans son cœur» (p. 37: 30-31). This is followed by the narrator's justificatory use of *il estoit difficile*: «il estoit difficile qu'ils ne se plussent infiniment» (p. 38: 8-9). The first time Mme de Clèves's love is given a name is in the narrator's explanation of why the Princess alone (along with Guise whose perception is sharpened by his own love) penetrates the motives of Nemours's changed behavior: «elle auroit eu peine à s'en apercevoir elle-mesme, si l'*inclination* qu'elle avoit pour lui ne lui eust donné une attention particulière pour ses [Nemours's] actions, qui ne lui permît pas d'en douter» (p. 46: 27-30). The noun is then used to designate Mme de Chartres's perception of her daughter's feelings (p. 47: 5, 7). *Inclination* is also the name Mme de Chartres gives to this emotion in her last interview with Mme de Clèves (p. 56: 1, 5). The narrator used the same word in describing the Princess' state after Nemours's first visit: «L'*inclination* qu'elle avoit pour ce prince luy donnoit un trouble dont elle n'estoit pas maîtresse» (p. 77: 6-8). It then becomes, so to speak, part of the character's own lexicon: «elle fit réflexion à la violence de l'*inclination* qui l'entraînoit vers M. de Nemours» (p. 88: 19-20). From this point on, *inclination* often appears in passages of the heroine's interiority (15).

The way in which *inclination* is initially used to designate the heroine's feelings helps show her lack of complicity. Its use is crucial to an understanding of Mme de Clèves's attitude toward her husband: «elle n'avoit aucune *inclination* particulière pour sa personne» (p. 31: 3-4). Other occurrences of the noun offer no particular anomalies (16).

*Sentiment* might be called the equivalent of *chose* within the subgroup of the language of passion. Occurring seventy-three times, it is more frequent than either *amour* or *inclination*. Like *chose*, it is used to concretize («il [M. de Clèves] avoit eu pour elle [Mlle de Chartres] tous les *sentimens* de respect et d'estime qui lui estoient deûs,» p. 21: 23-25) or to attenuate («M. de Clèves ne trouva pas que Mlle de Chartres eust changé de *sentiment* en changeant de nom,» p. 33: 20-21). It is also often associated with the vocabulary of dissimulation and appearance (e.g. p. 6: 17; 24: 34-25: 1).

More elliptical than *inclination, sentiment* is used in the description of the Princess' first real consciousness of the nature of her feelings for Nemours. When her jealousy is stirred by Mme de Chartres's story of the Duke's supposed love for the Reine Dauphine, the Princess «vid alors que les *sentimens* qu'elle avoit pour lui [Nemours] estoient ceux que M. de Clèves luy avoit tant demandez» (p. 53: 8-10).

There is extensive literature available on the concept of love in *La Princesse de Clèves*. A further multiplication of examples of the ways in which sentimental vocabulary is used in the novel would still lead us to the same conclusion, as do these brief comments. Mme de Lafayette's uses of individual lexical items conform to the usage of her era (see Sigaux, pp. xxiii-iv). Focusing attention on the presentation of Mme de Clèves's love has shown that the choice and distribution of these items reflect, on a smaller scale, the shaping of perspective discussed in Part I of this study.

Not only does the reader watch Mme de Clèves's perception of her feelings become gradually clearer, but he is also persuaded not to condemn her for them. These two aspects of the novel are illustrated by the uses of *inclination* and *passion*, respectively.

The reader's perception is also ironic because he is given the privileges of insight into the other characters and of observing the heroine from the outside. This facet of *La Princesse de Clèves* may be seen in the use of *passion* to describe Nemours's feelings and in the narrator's use of the word in reference to the Princess, before the character herself uses *passion*. Thus, one again finds evidence of the twin components of the reader's perspective, complicity and irony.

# CONCLUSION

The fascination exercised by *La Princesse de Clèves* is manifest in the world of French letters. Yet, the attraction the novel holds clearly derives from much more than a mere contrast between this work's shape and language and those of later novels. *La Princesse de Clèves* could not have called forth such diverse reactions on the grounds of difference alone. While, certainly, some aspects of its language (the frequency of *chose*, for example) and style do give the novel an air of its age, they neither cripple nor impoverish it.

The richness of *La Princesse de Clèves*'s tradition testifies amply that the novel, so «simple,» so «poor» in appearance, carries within it the capacity to convey that «pity beyond all telling» which Yeats finds at the heart of love. The conceptual world reflected in the ironic patterns of those words relating to «truth,» the changing points of view, the narrator's explicitness or reticence, the characters' speech or silence—all these serve to articulate the *indicible* in what Alain Niderst has so well called «le roman paradoxal.»

I have sought to find keys to some of the novel's fascination through an examination of narrative strategies. These strategies create, for the reader, a perspective composed of complicity and irony. By involving the reader with the heroine and her destiny, by making him share her optic, Mme de Lafayette creates a rapport between reader and character implied in Racine's term *toucher*. Irony provides the reader with the distance necessary to that pleasurable esthetic contemplation described by *plaire*. Thus, in *La Princesse de Clèves*, Mme de Lafayette attains the classical ideal, *plaire et toucher*.

# NOTES

# PREFACE

1. Maurice Laugaa, *Lectures de Madame de Lafayette* (Paris: Colin, 1971), provides a convenient survey of major *Princesse de Clèves* criticism from the novel's publication through the 1960's.

2. «A Structural Stylistic Analysis of *La Princesse de Clèves*,» Diss. Columbia, 1971 (cited hereafter as Tiefenbrun); «Analytische Dialektik in der *Princesse de Clèves*,» *Poetica*, 5 (1972), 183-90; «The Art of Repetition in *La Princesse de Clèves*,» *Modern Language Review*, 68 (1973), 40-50.

3. Cf. Wolfgang Iser, *The Implied Reader* (Baltimore and London: Johns Hopkins University Press, 1974), pp. 274-94.

4. A modified form of the concepts of collocation and set can be applied specifically to the vocabulary of the novel, allowing the interactions of words, and the context, to elucidate dictionary definitions. See John Spencer and Michael Gregory, «An Approach to the Study of Style,» in *Linguistics and Style*, Nils E. Enkvist, John Spencer and Michael Gregory (Oxford: Oxford University Press, 1964), pp. 72-74 et passim.

# PART I

# INTRODUCTION

1. Marie-Madeleine de Lafayette, *La Princesse de Clèves*, ed. Emile Magne (Geneva: Droz, and Lille: Giard, 1950), p. 73: 6-20. Unless otherwise indicated, all references are to this edition. Each reference includes page number followed by line number. There are thirty-five lines on a full page of text.

2. Following the more subtle distinctions made by Marcel Muller, *Les Voix narratives dans la «Recherche du temps perdu»* (Geneva: Droz, 1965), p. 8, the writer who, as artist, speaks through the whole of his work is differentiated from the narrator, one of the writer's creations. (Second references to all critical works will be included in the text.)

3. A detailed explication of this passage is found in Part I, Chapter II.

4. See especially Francillon, pp. 92-116, 207-14; Jean Rousset, *«La Princesse de Clèves,»* in *Forme et signification* (Paris: Corti, 1962), pp. 17-44 (cited hereafter as Rousset); Alain Niderst, *La Princesse de Clèves, le roman paradoxal* (Paris: Larousse, 1973), pp. 76-80, et passim; Barbara R. Woshinsky, *«La Princesse de Clèves»; The Tension of Elegance* (Paris and The Hague: Mouton, 1973), et passim; Helen K. Kaps, *Moral Perspective in «La Princesse de Clèves»* (Eugene, Oregon: University of Oregon Books, 1968), pp. 46-64, et passim. While Francillon treats both perspective and point of view, his use of these concepts, and the results obtained, differ substantially from my own.

5. Malcolm Bradbury, «Towards a Poetics of Fiction: An Approach through Structure,» *Novel*, 1 (1967), 52.

6. «The Place of Style in the Structure of the Text,» in *Literary Style: A Symposium*, ed. Seymour Chatman (London and New York: Oxford University Press, 1971), pp. 32-33.

7. «Les Catégories du récit littéraire,» *Communications*, 8 (1966), 146.

8. *A Study of Literature for Readers and Critics* (Ithaca, New York: Cornell University Press, 1943), p. 63. Cf. Wayne C. Booth, *The Rhetoric of Fiction* (Chicago: University of Chicago Press, 1961), p. 112.

# CHAPTER I

1. Marie-Madeleine de Lafayette, *Lettres de Madame de Lafayette au Chevalier de Lescheraine: Texte provenant des Archives de Turin,* ed. Jean de Bazin (Paris: Nizet, 1970), p. 1.

2. «Le malheur de Saint-Quentin avoit diminué l'espérance de nos conquestes,» p. 14: 20-21.

3. E.g. «Mme Elizabeth de France . . . commençoit à faire paraître un esprit surprenant et cette incomparable beauté *qui luy a esté si funeste,»* p. 7: 7-10, my emphasis. See also pp. 5: 2; 8: 8; 27: 16-19; 93: 7-13; 119: 14-31. (Unless otherwise indicated, emphasis will be mine in all quotations from *La Princesse de Clèves.*)

4. [Jean-Antoine de Charnes] *Conversations sur la Critique de La princesse de Clèves* (Paris: Barbin, 1679), pp. 129-30.

5. E.g., the comments on Mme de Valentinois's manner of dress, pp. 5: 14-6: 3, or the description of Saint-André, pp. 13:27-14: 8.

6. Claudette Sarlet, «La Description des personnages dans *La Princesse de Clè-*

*ves,*» *XVIIe Siècle,* 44 (1959), 191, says that the description of Mlle de Chartres is an apparition and not a portrait. See also Niderst, p. 43.

7. Woshinsky, p. 108, writes, «During this whole opening movement of the novel, Mlle de Chartres is presented as the perfect social object, adorned for others' gaze, without any apparent life of her own.»

8. «Il avoit . . . un air dans toute sa personne qui faisoit qu'*on* ne pouvoit regarder que luy dans tous les lieux où il paraissoit,» pp. 10: 16-11: 4.

9. Cf. William O. Goode, «A Mother's Goals in *La Princesse de Clèves*: Worldly and Spiritual Distinction,» *Neophilologus,* 56 (1972), 398-406.

10. Woshinsky, pp. 104-05, points out that *vertu,* p. 17: 9, is first used in connection with Mme de Chartres, while the generalization quoted above indirectly condemns those who do not share Mme de Chartres's opinions.

11. Jan Mukařovský, «Standard Language and Poetic Language,» in *Essays in the Language of Literature,* eds. Seymour Chatman and Samuel Levin (Boston: Houghton Mifflin, 1967), p. 242 writes, «Foregrounding is the opposite of automatization of an act; the more an act is automatized the less it is consciously executed; the more it is foregrounded, the more completely conscious does it become.» In this study the term is used to designate the techniques by which the reader's attention is called to a particular word or passage. Here, the contrast created by the intrusion of direct discourse calls attention to the passages thus presented. This notion of contrast with preceding context is influenced by Riffaterre's definition of a stylistic device: «Criteria for Style Analysis,» *Word,* 15 (1959), 154-74, and «Stylistic Context,» *Word,* 16 (1960), 207-18.

12. Cf. Francillon, p. 31, on the use of *il fallut* in *Montpensier* to translate the ineluctable nature of Chabannes's love.

13. Retroactive irony occurs essentially upon rereading, when knowledge of the outcome enables the reader to perceive the ways in which elements which appeared normal on a first reading actually laid the foundation for the *dénouement.*

14. Jules Brody, «*La Princesse de Clèves* and the Myth of Courtly Love,» *University of Toronto Quarterly,* 38 (1969), 131-32.

15. As both Rousset, p. 43, and Niderst, p. 52, state, the Princess is indeed the central consciousness of the novel. While each critic offers an explanation of the modifications this structure undergoes, neither gives much consideration to the effect this aspect of *La Princesse de Clèves* has on the reader.

16. «*Mme de Clèves ne faisoit pas semblant d'entendre ce que disoit le prince de Condé; mais elle l'écoutoit avec attention.* Elle jugeoit aisément quelle part elle avoit à l'opinion que soutenoit M. de Nemours, et sur tout à ce qu'il disoit du chagrin de n'estre pas au bal où estoit sa maîtresse, parce qu'il ne devoit pas estre à celuy du Mareschal de Saint-André, et que le Roy l'envoyoit au-devant du Duc de Ferrare,» p. 49: 3-10.

17. *L'Art de l'analyse dans la Princesse de Clèves* (Paris: Ophrys, 1970), p. 38; cf. Niderst, p. 71.

18. Here and in Chapter III, the use of direct discourse is analyzed in terms of narrative strategy. Niderst, pp. 158-60, feels that the structuring of direct discourse is dictated by a conflict between life and intellect, which is seen both in the Princess' story, and in the author's attempts to control and structure her material. However, any such identification between the heroine's *éducation sentimentale* and Mme de Lafayette's esthetic struggle assumes a view of art which did not arise until much later, and ignores the usefulness of the particular structures chosen in determining the

reader's perspective. There is little point in speculating on Mme de Lafayette's attitude toward those choices.

19. Approximately 31% of Part I (511 of 1634 lines) is in direct discourse. Because she presents the initial situation, the narrator plays a greater role in Part I than in the rest of the novel. Of this, approximately 19% is composed of tales and framing conversations; 12% is plot-advancing, as opposed to plot-enriching. 64% of Part II (1000 of 1587 lines) is in direct discourse. The «digressions,» as well as the tourney announcement and the letter (both of which have the same foregrounding effect), constitute 44%. 20% is plot-advancing. In Part III, 689, or 42% of the 1651 lines are in direct discourse, with only 9% consisting in tales and framing; 33% is plot-advancing. Part IV contains no tales, and 506, or 33% of the 1549 lines, are in direct discourse. The relationship between the above distribution and plot-structure is direct. Douglas R. Hall, «A Structural Analysis of the Fictional Works of Madame de La Fayette,» Diss. University of Maryland, 1968, pp. 59-61, 68, 174, gives statistics on the proportions of monologue, dialogue, description, narration, historicity, and analysis for the four fictional works.

20. See for example Tzvetan Todorov, *Littérature et signification* (Paris: Larousse, 1967), pp. 79-81.

21. E.g., p. 53: 5-16. Techniques used to translate interiority will be treated in Chapter II.

22. «By his needle he understands ironia, That with one eye looks in two ways at once,» Thomas Middleton and W. Rowley, *A courtly masque: the device called the world tost at tennis (1620)*, in *OED*, s.v. «irony.»

23. For a different view of the narrator's functions, see Francillon, pp. 207-14.

# CHAPTER II

1. The punctuation of the original edition (Paris: Barbin, 1678) is used in citing passages to be closely explicated on the assumption that it is closer to the author's intention. References to this edition will be indicated by P1678 followed by volume and page numbers.

2. Robert Humphrey, *Stream of Consciousness in the Modern Novel* (Berkeley, Los Angeles and London: University of California Press, 1954), pp. 4, 62-84.

3. On the use of *poison* in reference to *passion* in *Phèdre*, see Robert W. Hartle, «Racine's Hidden Metaphors,» *Modern Language Notes*, 76 (1961), 137-38. On the use of *poison* in *La Princesse de Clèves*, see Rosemarie Burkart, *Die Kunst des Masses in Mme de Lafayette's «Princesse de Clèves»* (Bonn and Köln: Röhrscheid, 1933), p. 162.

4. Niderst, p. 78, speaks of «un langage neutre, mi-objectif, mi-subjectif,» used in dealing with interiority; cf. Francillon, p. 123.

5. This construction parallels the use of *il estoit difficile . . . sans / de ne pas*

used as a means of justifying intervention in Part I.

6. The word *passion* has not yet been applied to the heroine's love, except once in a form weakened by its placement and the indefinite plural: «elle pensoit que ce charme qu'elle trouvoit dans sa vue estoit le commencement des passions,» p. 55: 23-25.

7. Jean Dubois, René Lagane and Alain Lerond, *Dictionnaire du français classique* (Paris: Larousse, 1971), s.v. «tendresse,» suggest «Attendrissement, émotion.» This dictionary will be referred to hereafter as Dubois.

8. Marcel Cressot, *Le Style et ses techniques: Précis d'analyse stylistique*, 3rd ed. (Paris: Presses Universitaires de France, 1956), p. 168, uses the term *cadence majeure* to describe the tendency, dictated by reasons of logic and musicality, to arrange a sentence by elements of increasing length.

9. Cressot, p. 32, points out that the reader is never without a minimum consciousness of the oral aspects of the written material.

10. Cf. Tiefenbrun, pp. 66-67, as well as her «Analytische Dialektik,» pp. 186-88.

11. Whereas Fabre, *L'Art de l'analyse*, p. 43, and Marie-Jeanne Durry, «Le Monologue intérieur dans *La Princesse de Clèves*,» in *La Littérature narrative d'imagination* (Paris: Presses Universitaires de France, 1959), p. 91, both deny an effort on Mme de Lafayette's part to imitate emotional phrasing, Peter Nurse, *Classical Voices: Studies of Corneille, Racine, Molière, Madame de Lafayette* (London: Harrap, 1971), p. 206, is more helpful in noting the intensity achieved by «allowing the reader to experience directly the emotion by analyzing the factors and the situation which give rise to it. In this way, we share the perspective of the novel's protagonists and supply from ourselves the emotional content of their experiences and thoughts.»

12. *Horreur* is used four times in the novel, p. 69: 3, here, p. 177: 4, and p. 180: 2; *horrible* once, p. 191: 34. Four of the five uses refer directly to jealousy and its effects. The fifth, p. 180: 2, describes the way the heroine feels about herself when she sees herself as the cause of the Prince's death. The word is reserved for the most violent situations. Tiefenbrun, pp. 59-60, discusses the way in which, in this last instance, p. 180: 2, the sentence, arranged by postposition and accumulation, puts full weight on *horreur*. On the consubstantiality of love and jealousy in Mme de Lafayette's other works, see Francillon, pp. 60, 82.

13. Cressot, p. 7, «L'expressionisme reconstitue logiquement les faits fournis par la sensation; il les classe selon un rapport de cause à effet, alors que l'impressionisme nous livre les faits tels que les fournit une perception immédiate.»

14. Cf. Niderst, p. 68, whose assessment of free indirect style ignores the function of irony.

15. Jean Fabre, «Bienséance et sentiment chez Mme de Lafayette,» *CAIEF*, 11 (1959), 40.

16. Brody deals extensively with this question: «In *La Princesse de Clèves* the role of the courtly ideal coincides exactly with its ritual function as an element in culture: to absorb the known ugliness and baseness of men's motives into a sublime sentimental vision. And Mme de Clèves' essential problem consists in ascertaining just how far or how deep this process of absorption or sublimation can reasonably be expected to go,» p. 118.

# CHAPTER III

1. As noted above, 42% of Part III is in direct discourse, while only 9% of this represents tales and their framing conversations. On dialogue and monologue, cf. Francillon, pp. 218-21.

2. In her soliloquies, Mme de Clèves uses *M. de Nemours* and *il* but not *ce prince*. Cf. Claudette Delhez-Sarlet, «Style indirect libre et 'point de vue' dans *La Princesse de Clèves*,» *Cahiers d'Analyse Textuelle*, 6 (1964), 77.

3. I do not wish to imply that Mme de Clèves's confession was an act of unmixed heroism, only that her desire to find such self-denial in her husband is doomed to failure. The Prince's view of the situation is more realistic: «Vous avez raison, madame, reprit-il, je suis injuste. Refusez-moi toutes les fois que je vous demanderay de pareilles choses; mais ne vous offencez pourtant pas, si je vous les demande,» p. 128: 28-31. See Woshinsky, pp. 99-102, for an analysis of the anti-social implications of the *aveu*.

4. See Booth, pp. 78-79; Marcel Arland, «Madame de La Fayette et la *Princesse de Clèves*,» in *Les Echanges* (Paris: Gallimard, 1946), p. 99.

5. Treated here in detail are the 'balanced views' discussed briefly in Chapter I. When Bernard Pingaud, *Madame de La Fayette par elle-même* (Paris: Seuil, 1959), p. 89, writes «On parle beaucoup dans les romans de Mme de La Fayette, mais jamais de ce qui importe,» he points up the constraints which prevent open communication among the characters. The reader's interest in what *is* said in direct discourse is increased by virtue of his ironic penetration of the character's words.

6. See especially Tiefenbrun, pp. 49-51; Kaps, pp. 3-12, 72-76; Rousset, pp. 25-27; Michel Butor, «Sur 'La Princesse de Clèves,'» *Répertoire* (Paris: Editions de Minuit, 1960), pp. 74-78; Francillon, pp. 111-12.

7. In the same way the discreet comment at the end of the subsequent bit of narration («peut-estre que des regards et des paroles obligeantes n'eussent pas tant augmenté l'amour de M. de Nemours que faisoit cette conduite austère,» p. 133: 25-28) foreshadows Mme de Clèves's assertion in the renunciation («je croy mesme que les obstacles ont fait vostre constance,» p. 192: 16-17).

8. Jean-Baptiste de Valincour, *Lettres à Madame la Marquise *** sur le sujet de la Princesse de Clèves*, ed. Albert Cazes (Paris: Bossard, 1925), p. 115.

9. Many critics have commented on the dramatic aspect of the novel. While the essential differences between the genres and their modes of perception should never be forgotten, those aspects of *La Princesse de Clèves* studied in this section do present analogies with drama. See, for example, Raymond Picard, *Two Centuries of French Literature*, trans. John Cairncross (New York and Toronto: McGraw-Hill, 1969-70), p. 122; Isabelle McNeill, «L'Univers dramatique de Madame de La Fayette,» Diss. Stanford, 1970; Jacques Vier, *Littérature à l'emporte-pièce*, 5th series (Paris: Les Editions du Cèdre, 1969), p. 38.

## CHAPTER IV

1. After the confession, the narrator did not hesitate to affirm «Jamais mary n'avoit eu une passion si violente pour sa femme, et ne l'avoit tant estimée,» p. 131: 10-12.

2. Except for the terse treatment of his death, p. 179: 17-21, the subsequent passages dealing with the Prince are all in direct discourse.

3. As M. de Clèves puts it, partially overstating the case, «vous connoîtrez la différence d'estre aimée, comme je vous aimois, à l'estre par des gens qui, en vous témoignant de l'amour, ne cherchent que l'honneur de vous séduire,» p. 177: 19-22.

4. Brody, pp. 111-12, says that, while Mme de Lafayette stresses Nemours's «essential sincerity,» even for the reader, who knows more than Mme de Clèves, the character never emerges with total clarity. This situation correlates with the goal of having the reader share the heroine's perspective and with Brody's analysis, p. 118, of Mme de Clèves's essential problem.

5. Cf. Georges Kassaï, «L'Indirect dans la 'Princesse de Clèves,'» Lettres Nouvelles, (1970), 123-27.

6. A similar result is achieved through the presentation of the letter-forging without any direct or indirect reproduction of the repartee between Nemours and Mme de Clèves, pp. 118: 17-119: 9. Likewise, in the final scene with M. de Clèves, the passing over of the Princess' actual description of the night at Coulommiers, p. 176: 1-6, not only avoids repetition, but also prevents the reader from drawing any conclusions as to her level of consciousness at that time.

7. Cf. David I. Grossvogel, Limits of the Novel (Ithaca, N.Y.: Cornell University Press, 1968), pp. 126, 135.

8. Peut-être is used similarly several times in Part IV. When informing the reader about the paintings Mme de Clèves took to Coulommiers, the narrator said, «Il y avoit entr'autres le siège de Metz, et tous ceux qui s'y estoient distinguez estoient peints fort ressemblans. M. de Nemours estoit de ce nombre et c'estoit peut-estre ce qui avoit donné envie à Mme de Clèves d'avoir ces tableaux,» p. 163: 25-30. Likewise, in the pavilion scene, describing the Princess' reaction, the narrator comments, «Peut-estre souhaitoit-elle, autant qu'elle le craignoit, d'y trouver M. de Nemours,» p. 169: 10-11.

9. Tiefenbrun offers a highly developed treatment of the isomorphic elements of the plot in the second half of her dissertation, pp. 70-127.

10. On the nature of this refusal, see Maurice Léo, «La Rhétorique de l'obstacle surmonté chez Corneille et chez Madame de Lafayette,» in Missions et démarches de la critique: Mélanges offerts au Professeur Jacques Vier (Paris: Klincksieck, 1973), pp. 725-31.

11. See Tiefenbrun, p. 48; Gabriel Bounoure, «Les Mille Oiseaux du silence, II. La perle blanche,» Mercure de France, 352 (1964), 426-35; Woshinsky, pp. 38-47; Francillon, pp. 169-71.

12. As Nemours senses he is losing the argument, his reasons become less and less lofty, until finally he questions Mme de Clèves's ability to resist, saying, «Il est plus difficile que vous ne pensez, madame, de résister à ce qui nous plaist et à ce qui nous aime,» p. 193: 29-31. It is in lieu of what would have been Nemours's subse-

quent response that the narrator intervenes.

# PART II

# INTRODUCTION

1. E.g. Claudette Delhez-Sarlet, «Une Page de *La Princesse de Clèves*,» *Cahiers d'Analyse Textuelle*, 3 (1961), 65; Charles Dédéyan, *Madame de Lafayette* (Paris: Société d'Edition d'Enseignement Supérieur, 1955), p. 251; Woshinsky, p. 62.

2. On these points, see, for example, Hippolyte Taine, «Mme de La Fayette— *La Princesse de Clèves*,» in *Essais de critique et d'histoire*, 16th ed. (Paris: Hachette, 1920), p. 248; Jean Cocteau, «Préface,» in Mme de Lafayette, *La Princesse de Clèves, La Comtesse de Tende, La Princesse de Montpensier, Lettres et mémoires* (Paris: Nelson, 1958), p. xviii; Fabre, «Bienséance et sentiment,» pp. 40-43; Fabre, *L'Art de l'analyse*, pp. 33, 44, 70; Burkart, pp. 156-57.

# CHAPTER I

1. As concretized in Mme de Chartres's apothegm: «Si vous jugez sur les apparences en ce lieu-cy . . . vous serez souvent trompée: ce qui paroist n'est presque jamais la vérité,» pp. 39: 35-40: 2. Cf. Tiefenbrun, p. 129; Niderst, pp. 55-59, 177; Kaps, pp. 5-7.

2. I have made extensive use of Jean de Bazin, *Index du vocabulaire de La Princesse de Clèves* (Paris: Nizet, 1967). In the course of my investigations, I have encountered a number of errors and omissions in Bazin's work. This should explain any disparities in word counts. I have also studied a number of terms which Bazin either does not list at all, or for which he gives only a total.

3. Although on one level, the verb *paraître* in the second quotation merely means «arrived,» the fact that absolute synonymy does not exist makes it unlikely that the reader is wholly insensitive to the difference in connotation between *il parut* and *il arriva* or *il vint*.

4. Antoine Furetière, *Dictionnaire universel contenant généralement tous les mots françois tant vieux que modernes*, Nouvelle édition corrigée et augmentée (Rot-

terdam: Leers, 1694), s.v. «vérité,» «Certitude d'une chose qui est toûjours la même, qui ne change point . . . se prend aussi pour la connoissance d'une chose telle qu'elle est effectivement . . . se dit aussi des connoissances dont on decouvre la certitude par art.» See also, *Dictionnaire de l'Académie françoise* (Paris: Coignard, 1694), s.v. «vray.»

5. Paul Zumthor, «Le Sens de l'amour et du mariage dans la conception classique de l'homme (Mme de la Fayette),» *Archiv für das Studium der neueren Sprachen und Literaturen*, 181, new series 81 (1942), 104, feels that the heightened perception sometimes occasioned by love (*amour-passion*) makes this latter an even greater threat to reason since this love is not totally blind. As I hope to show here and below, the essential problem is one of instability and uncertainty, and not of emotion simply either deceiving or informing.

6. Pages 51: 19; 51: 32; 54: 6; 62: 31; 73: 19; 79: 19; 82: 4; 103: 2; 104: 24; 110: 6; 113: 23; 114: 11; 114: 32; 115: 10; 116: 12; 119: 13; 127: 10; 129: 9; 137: 15; 154: 10; 161: 24; 162: 35; 178: 23; 179: 4; 180: 16.

7. Among the examples given, *Académie*, s.v. «vray,» «*chercher la verité. advoüer la verité.*»

8. The difference in the narrator's attitude toward Mme de Clèves's relations with Nemours and with her husband can be seen in the two generalizations; the former underlines her complicity, the latter her veracity.

9. See M. de Clèves's reproach to his wife, «Vous n'avez pu me dire la *vérité* toute entière, vous m'en avez caché la plus grande partie,» p. 161: 23-25.

10. The only exception is Nemours's partial discovery of the real story of M. de Clèves's death: «il devina une partie de la *vérité*,» p. 180: 15-16.

11. Eight of twenty-three occurrences of *véritable*; six with *passion* and one each with *attachement* and *affliction*: pp. 63: 19; 68: 33; 75: 20; 76: 27; 141: 30; 176: 16; 177: 17; 187: 22. Excluded from the present discussion are the two instances of the locution *il est véritable*, pp. 127: 16-17; 190: 8. They will be treated with *il est vrai*. The other occurrences of *véritable* are: pp. 22: 22; 25: 12; 43: 33; 73: 35; 79: 29; 79: 34; 108: 25; 114: 26; 134: 29; 140: 10; 142: 13; 154: 9; 189: 35.

12. Of the one hundred and twelve uses of *passion* in the novel, only six are modified by *véritable*. Two of these occur in the Sancerre episode, pp. 63: 19; 68: 33, while the other four relate to the protagonists, pp. 75: 20; 141: 30; 177: 17; 187: 22.

13. *Véritable*, when not used as a predicate adjective, is only postposed in one other instance, when M. de Clèves describes himself as «un homme qui vous aimoit d'une passion véritable et légitime,» p. 177: 17-18. Here again one encounters a case of accrued meaning.

14. In addition to the three examples below, see pp. 11: 14; 30: 23; 51: 22; 106: 9.

15. If, as for *vérité* and *véritable*, one follows the procedure of examining the first occurrences of *véritablement*, one finds the same gradual undermining of meaning. The first occurrence deals on the most simple level with passion and dissimulation. The narrator says of Nemours, «il estoit difficile de deviner celle qu'il aimoit *véritablement*,» p. 11: 13-14. In the next instance, the distortion of perception by love is made explicit. Mlle de Chartres «fut *véritablement* touchée de reconnoissance du procédé du Prince de Clèves,» p. 30: 23-24, and her real gratitude gives rise to a false interpretation, p. 30: 24-29. In the third case, *véritablement* is used in an explicit lie when Mme de Chartres assures the Reine Dauphine that her daughter did not

attend Saint-André's ball because, «Elle estoit *véritablement* malade,» p. 51: 22-23.

16. Emile Littré, *Dictionnaire de la langue française*, éd. intégrale (Paris: Gallimard-Hachette, 1970), s.v. «vraisemblable» and «vraisemblance.»

17. *Vraisemblance* appears twice more: pp. 133: 22-23; 145: 30. *Vraisemblable* is used seven times: pp. 79: 33; 114: 8; 121: 9; 139: 9; 145: 3; 172: 7; 179: 5. For the reader aware of Henri II's fate, the first occurrence of the adjective is ironic. In discussing predictions, the King says, «on m'a dit tant de choses fausses et si peu *vraysemblables* que je suis demeuré convaincu que l'on ne peut rien sçavoir de véritable,» p. 79: 32-34. Since this is immediately followed by his account of the prediction, the perception of retroactive irony, *even on a first reading*, is highly probable.

18. When Mme de Clèves objects to her husband's criticism of Mme de Tournon, saying that he has often called her one of the most estimable women at court, the Prince replies, «Il est *vray* . . . mais les femmes sont incompréhensibles et, quand je les voy toutes, je me trouve si heureux de vous avoir que je sçaurois assez admirer mon bonheur,» p. 58: 23-26. The locations of *vrai* are: pp. 8: 15; 29: 8; 31: 21; 31: 33; 38: 1; 38: 25; 54: 15; 58: 23; 76: 5; 113: 14; 125: 10; 128: 17; 139: 16; 140: 7; 173: 17; 174: 29; 189: 19; 195: 3.

19. Pages 31: 33; 54: 14-15; 58: 23; 113: 14; 128: 17; 139: 16; 140: 7.

20. Burkart, p. 155, cites François de Callières, «Les Mots à la mode» (1692), who treats *il est vrai que* as «expression vide de sens qu'emploient sans cesse les dames de la Cour et de la Ville ainsi que les Courtisans.»

21. Le Roi de Navarre «excelloit dans la guerre, et le Duc de Guise luy donnoit une émulation qui l'avoit porté plusieurs fois à quitter sa place de général, pour aller combattre auprès de luy comme un simple soldat, dans les lieux les plus périlleux. *Il est vray* aussi que ce Duc avoit donné des marques d'une valeur si admirable . . . ,» p. 8: 11-17.

22. This is one of the things upon which the character prides himself: «vous [Nemours] avez veu que ma conduite n'a pas esté réglée par mes sentimens,» p. 189: 7-9. In another sense, of course, this statement is ironic since all Mme de Clèves's behavior has been dictated by her attempts to deal with her feelings.

23. *Certitude* is twice used in the plural in the sense of evidence, pp. 147: 28; 170: 26. These uses do not play a role in the ironic structuring under discussion.

24. «Est-il possible que l'amour m'ait si absolument osté la raison et la hardiesse et qu'il m'ait rendu si différent de ce que j'ay esté dans les autres passions de ma vie?» p. 185: 17-20.

25. On Mme de Clèves's *certitude*, see particularly Brody, pp. 128-30, as well as Bertrand D'Astorg, «Le Refus de Madame de Clèves,» *Esprit*, 31 (1963), 661.

26. *Académie*, s.v. «certain,» gives as its first definition, «Asseuré, vray. *Faire un rapport certain & asseuré de quelque chose. des nouvelles certaines.*» Furetière and Dubois give similar definitions.

27. The Queen's action, «elle le [the Vidame] perdit ensuitte à la conjuration d'Amboise,» p. 119: 30, serves the same function in the passage discussed in the preceding paragraph.

28. «L'ambition et la galanterie étoient l'âme de cette cour,» p. 23: 18-19.

29. Earlier in the scene, the Princess uses the adverb in much the same way: «je me repentirai *infailliblement* de vous l' [her complaisance] avoir accordée,» p. 187: 13-14. Like the ironic structure involving *certitude*, the adjective and adverb are used in contexts where the characters' certainty is borne out by events, and where it is not, pp. 93: 12; 100: 28; 118: 5; 172: 15; 187: 6, culminating in the Princess'

two usages discussed here.

30. The literature on this point is extensive. Typical are: Stirling Haig, *Madame de Lafayette* (New York: Twayne Publishers, 1970), p. 115; Sylvère Lotringer, «La Structuration romanesque,» *Critique*, 277 (1970), 504, 511, and «Le Roman impossible,» *Poétique*, 1.3 (1970), 298; Pierre Van Rutten, «Style et signification dans *La Princesse de Clèves*,» *Le Français dans le Monde*, 36 (1968), 17; Robert N. Nicolich, «The Language of Vision in *La Princesse de Clèves*: The Baroque Principle of Control and Release,» *Language and Style*, 4 (1971), 282-83.

31. Not discussed above are the eight occurrences of *certain* in anteposition. A comparison of the definitions and examples found in Dubois, Furetière, and *Académie*, shows that in anteposition *certain* might denote either certainty or indetermination. The meaning of each of these is clarified by context and by the shaping of perspective as described in the first part of this study. The eight instances in question are found on pp. 20: 17; 30: 25-26; 31: 34; 37: 19; 64: 23; 81: 31; 154: 15; 183: 1.

32. See, respectively, Kaps, p. 85; Bernard Laudy, «La Vision tragique de Mme de La Fayette, ou un jansénisme athée,» *Revue de l'Institut de Sociologie de l'Université Libre de Bruxelles*, 3 (1969), 459; Brody, pp. 128-34; Lotringer, «La Structuration,» p. 517; Zumthor, p. 106.


# CHAPTER II


1. E.g. Tiefenbrun, «The Art,» p. 47. In her dissertation, pp. 27-28, 38, 83, 129, she holds that the express refusal of mimesis (the *indicible*) serves to underline one half of the pair Mimesis/Refusal of Mimesis, a variant of the opposition Exterior/Interior, one of the four major binary structures around which she contends the novel is organized.

2. *La Princesse de Clèves, La Princesse de Montpensier* (Paris: Colin, 1960), p. xxiv.

3. The six other occurrences of *presque* are of little individual interest. All serve not to avoid or to attenuate but simply to describe adequately. E.g. «ce qui paroist n'est *presque* jamais la vérité,» p. 40: 2. The other instances may be found on pp. 54: 35; 152: 21; 153: 30-31; 176: 6-7; 179: 18-19.

4. Littré, s.v. «quasi,» tells us that «les puristes du XVIIe siècle déclaraient *quasi* un terme vieilli bien qu'employé par les meilleurs auteurs.» This may account for Valincour's criticism of the use of *quasi*, p. 256, «que je rencontre partout, et même dans des endroits où il choque l'oreille.» Twenty instances hardly accounts for Valincour's impression of high frequency, while the perception of each instance as a linguistic aberration would.

5. The other instances of *quasi* used in this way are found on pp. 28: 17; 30: 3; 60: 8; 63: 17; 67: 15; 74: 11; 76: 25; 87: 21; 87: 26; 103: 17; 124: 16; 133: 19; 133: 21; 163: 14; 169: 17; 179: 23.

6. An Interpretation also confirmed by the reappearance of the verb *plaire* a few lines below, in the narrator's explanatory generalization, «Les paroles les plus obscures d'un homme qui *plaist* donnent plus d'agitation que des déclarations ouvertes d'un homme qui ne *plaist* pas,» p. 77: 8-10.

7. Littré, and Paul Robert, *Dictionnaire alphabétique et analogique de la langue française* (Paris: Société du Nouveau Littré, 1966), s.v. «chose.»

8. There are a certain number of cases in which *quelque chose* is used in ways either rare in, or absent from, modern French, but which offer no particular stylistic interest: «il n'y avoit que *quelque chose* fort au-dessus d'elles qui pust m'engager,» p. 103: 18-19 (instead of *quelqu'une*); «Elle ne put s'empescher de luy en témoigner *quelque chose,*» p. 54: 7-8 and «par la crainte de vous importuner, ou de perdre *quelque chose* de votre estime,» p. 177: 11-12 (in the sense of *une partie*). It is also used twice in the negative sense of *rien*: «je ne pouvois m'imaginer qu'il y eust *quelque chose* de pire que la mort d'une maîtresse que l'on aime et dont on est aimé,» p. 66: 8-10; «je pense que dans un mariage Votre Majesté ne me conseilleroit pas de luy disputer *quelque chose,* p. 71: 25-26.

9. This parallels (but is motivated somewhat differently) Nemours's foregoing circumlocution, «Tout ce que je puis vous apprendre, madame, c'est que j'ay souhaité ardemment que vous n'eussiez pas avoué à M. de Clèves ce que vous me cachiez et que vous luy eussiez caché ce que vous m'eussiez laissé voir,» p. 188: 9-13.

10. Robert gives «intrigue» as one of the possible meanings of *quelque chose*.

11. See Part I, Chapter II, for an analogous observation on the paradoxical function of secondary mimesis.

12. This degree of explicitness does not come until late in the novel, after the Prince's death: «elle se faisoit un crime de n'avoir pas eu de la passion pour luy, comme si c'eust esté une chose qui eust esté en son pouvoir,» p. 181: 2-4.

13. See the anticipatory passage, p. 35: 12-20, «Il [Nemours] alla ensuite chez les Reines. Mme de Clèves n'y estoit pas, de sorte qu'elle ne le vid point . . . »

14. Pages 35: 34; 36: 3; see Part I, Chapter I.

15. «Elle lui loua M. de Nemours avec un certain air qui donna à Mme de Chartres la mesme pensée qu'avoit eue le Chevalier de Guise,» p. 37: 18-20.

16. These three plus pp. 31: 33-35; 33: 25-27, cited above.

17. The other instances of these usages may be found on pp. 68: 8-9; 95: 34-35; 138: 6-7; 141: 14; 143: 6.

18. Other examples of the use of *si peu* are found on pp. 119: 11 and 171: 29.

19. The repeated use of expressions of quantity actually continues further: «Il avoit *tant de* douceur et *tant de* disposition à la galanterie qu'il ne pouvoit refuser *quelques* soins à celles qui tâchoient de lui plaire,» p. 11: 9-12.

20. *Académie,* s.v. «peu,» is not particularly enlightening on this point: «*Si peu, Aussi-peu, Trop peu.* Façons de parler relatives & comparatives, dont on se sert en diverses phrases.» Furetière, s.v. «peu,» does not deal with the expression in a way relevant here.

21. Other instances of emphatic *si peu* are found on pp. 189: 3; 191: 16.

22. The courtly motif is carried out in the descriptions of Condé, «un petit corps *peu* favorisé de la nature,» p. 9: 9-10, of Mme de Valentinois, «*peu* de femmes lui estoient agréables,» p. 24: 12, and of Guise's relative poverty, «par le *peu* de bien qu'il avoit pour soutenir son rang,» p. 25: 4-5, and by the King's remark about his injury, «Il dit que c'estoit *peu* de chose,» p. 153: 11. On this expression, one finds in *Académie,* s.v. «peu,» «Quand on veut donner à entendre qu'on ne doit pas faire cas

d'une chose, d'une personne, on dit *C'est peu de chose.*»

23. The last part of the passage describes the two characters collectively: «Ils demeurèrent quelque temps sans se rien dire et se séparèrent sans avoir la force de se parler,» p. 136: 5-7.

24. Marie-Odile Sweetser, «*La Princesse de Clèves* et son unité,» *PMLA*, 87 (1972), 487 (cited hereafter as Sweetser), contrasts this passage with the description of Mme de Clèves at her husband's bedside, «le visage tout couvert de larmes,» p. 176: 12, calling the latter a manifestation of true despair at realizing too late how much her husband loved her, and the former a melancholy farewell to her youth and first love. Suffice it to say that Mme de Clèves's continued love for Nemours makes the interview a pleasurable as well as a painful experience, that it should be remembered that during the renunciation she is making a conscious effort to control both herself and the situation, and that the notion of a melancholy acceptance, if it is to be found at all in the novel, does not occur until the very end, pp. 199-201.

25. *Peu* appears five times in the locution *à peu près*, pp. 78: 13; 111: 15; 117: 26; 118: 4; 145: 23, presenting no particular interest. It is also used twice in the expression *il s'en fallait peu*, once in the Reine Dauphine's story of her mother, «*Il s'en falloit peu* mesme que ce manquement ne fist une rupture entre les deux Rois,» p. 29: 2-4, and once to describe the heroine's attitude towards her passion, «qu'elle pensoit que ce charme qu'elle trouvoit dans sa vue estoit le commencement des passions, *il s'en falloit peu* qu'elle ne crûst le haïr par la douleur que luy donnoit cette pensée,» p. 55: 23-26. In the latter case the more interesting element is the verb *croire*, which combines with the subordinating locution to convey the complexity of the Princess' feelings. On the use of *peu* in temporal indications, see section 8 below.

26. Robert, s.v. «guère,» «*Ne* . . . *guère* a un sens restrictif ou limitatif qui en fait (comme de 'pas beaucoup, pas très') l'expression atténuée de 'peu.'» He cites B. Lafaye, *Dictionnaire des synonymes de la langue française*, 2nd and 3rd eds. (Paris: Hachette, 1861 and 1903): «*Peu* est absolu, *guère* relatif.» Neither *Académie* nor Furetière, s.v. «guère,» give any indication of this distinction between *peu* and *guère*.

27. Pages 42: 23; 43: 34; 80: 13; 80: 16-17; 108: 11, respectively.

28. Other indicators of distance are the uses of *croire, s'imaginer, paraître* and the narrator's comments interspersed with the character's thoughts. For example: «Il estoit si éperdument amoureux d'elle qu'il croyoit que tout le monde avoit les mesmes sentimens. Il estoit véritable aussi qu'il avoit plusieurs rivaux; mais il s'en imaginoit encore davantage,» p. 127: 15-18.

29. Mme de Lafayette was capable of creating much more acerbic irony with *ne . . . guère*. In her *Vie de la Princesse d'Angleterre*, ed. Marie-Thérèse Hipp (Geneva: Droz, 1967), p. 56, one reads: «avant que de commencer cette rupture, elle avoit encore donné au comte de Guiche le moyen de voir Me pour chercher ensemble, disoit-elle, ceux de ne plus se voir. Ce n'est guère en présence que les personnes qui s'ayment trouvent ces sortes d'expediens; aussi cette conversation ne fit pas un grand effet, quoiqu'elle suspendît pour quelque temps le commerce des lettres.»

30. Pages 16: 17; 30: 11; 41: 23; 50: 33; 64: 2; 68: 19; 70: 35; 71: 13; 103: 3-4; 126: 25; 165: 16; 168: 28; 172: 7; 180: 6; 184: 12-13; 192: 17; 192: 19-20; 193: 29.

31. *Penser* appears as a euphemism for marriage or proposals on other occasions, e.g. «Mon devoir . . . me deffend de penser jamais à personne,» p. 189: 31-32.

32. Pages 13: 2; 41: 15; 58: 26; 64: 5-6; 95: 30; 127: 27; 128: 15; 159: 23;

174: 33.

33. Pages 61: 24; 64: 31; 102: 6; 108: 1.

34. The seventeen occurrences under discussion are found on pp. 19: 19; 35: 25; 46: 11; 47: 18-19; 47: 26; 75: 22; 75: 25-26; 81: 21; 113: 30; 122: 22; 130: 14; 130: 20; 166: 27; 183: 7; 198: 23-24; 199: 27; 201: 22.

35. The way in which the story and conversation are framed by descriptions of the lovers' passion, p. 38: 1-8 and p. 46: 3 ff., makes clear the thematic function of the «digression.» The digressions serve as outlines of the consequences of passion, as moral lessons or as unfulfilled potential courses for the Princess' passion. The literature on this point is extensive. Typical of the current tendency to see the episodes as integral parts of the novel rather than extraneous historical «padding» are: Picard, p. 115; Niderst, p. 145; Brody, p. 116; Fabre, *L'Art de l'analyse*, p. 37; Lotringer, «La Structuration,» p. 502. Haig, p. 123, sees the scene in which the *aveu* story is told as the «fifth» digression, showing how the heroine has come full circle. In the second half of her dissertation, Tiefenbrun demonstrates the integration of the various plot levels in the novel.

36. Interpreting *assez* as an intensifier would be out of keeping with the way in which the character is handled, combining favorable presentation with subtle undermining of this evaluation.

37. Critical opinion on the interpretation of this passage is divided. Brody, p. 123, sees Mme de Lafayette's condemnation as anticipating the Princess' disillusionment upon realizing that Nemours is indeed not exceptional. Niderst, p. 47, describes the act as excusable, but revealing of how passion can lead one to forget even the best interests of the beloved. See also Francillon, p. 208. For a contemporary reaction, see Valincour, p. 115.

38. Burkart, p. 160, contends that one must always «read into» *La Princesse de Clèves* in order to discover the intensity of the characters' emotions. On the contrary, that intensity is already literally *in* the novel's words, and the only time one is authorized to read in absent intensity is when the novel itself, as here, has created a context against which the fact and degree of understatement can be perceived.

39. *Oeuvres complètes*, eds. Jean Bruneau and Bernard Masson (Paris: Seuil, 1964), II, 160; cf. Arland, pp. 102-03.

40. For the thirty-one uses of *quelque* in temporal indications, as well as the six instances of *quelquefois*, see section 8.

41. Pages 20: 25; 35: 26; 35: 29; 57: 18; 64: 18; 102: 3; 104: 31; 114: 14; 133: 30; 139: 21; 143: 34; 144: 35; 145: 21; 167: 7; 169: 10; 179: 2; 183: 7; and pp. 64: 11; 93: 5; 134: 22; 144: 10; 145: 12, respectively.

42. As for the twenty-three occurrences of the locution *quelque... que*, their function is emphatic and, although this emphasis is grounded in extreme indefinition rather than extreme definition (as in most hyperbole), it is of only peripheral importance to the present discussion. The locution may be found on pp. 13: 23; 29: 5-6; 29: 15; 56: 17; 76: 16; 81: 29; 88: 34; 107: 1 (twice); 119: 14-15; 121: 26; 125: 16; 129: 18; 133: 25; 136: 31; 148: 6; 151: 11-12; 158: 16; 161: 16-17; 180: 21; 180: 31; 194: 14; 195: 29.

43. *En quelque sorte* appears twice more. It attenuates, for reasons which are self-evident. Sancerre says: «Si j'avois appris son [Mme de Tournon's] changement devant sa mort, la jalousie, la colère, la rage m'auroient rempli et m'auroient endurci *en quelque sorte* contre la douleur de sa perte,» p. 66: 26-29. In the confession, the Prince tells his wife: «Je m'estois consolé *en quelque sorte* de ne l' [her heart] avoir

pas touché par la pensée qu'il estoit incapable de l'estre,» p. 126: 16-18.

44. It is only afterwards, through her reaction to her mother's remarks about Nemours's relationship with the Reine Dauphine, that Mme de Clèves, through the first stirrings of jealousy, begins to admit the truth to herself, p. 53: 5-16.

45. Similar effects using just the adjective *quelque* may be found on pp. 32: 31; 54: 4.

46. There is one case in which the indetermination implied by *quelque* may simply be taken at face value: «Il [Nemours] envoya Lignerolles . . . pour voir les sentimens de la Reine [Elizabeth], et pour tascher de commencer *quelque* liaison,» p. 16: 24-27.

47. In many cases, it is virtually impossible to determine whether a particular passage should be considered indirect discourse or narration. While the concept of secondary mimesis represents an attempt to understand better certain of these passages by posing the question in terms more appropriate to a discussion of narrative strategy, its use is not intended to obscure the difficulty of making the narrative-indirect discourse distinction in efforts to treat specific lexical items according to their location in a particular sort of discourse, as is the case here.

48. Pages 48: 7; 48: 34; 60: 14; 81: 5; 88: 13; 107: 8; 114: 10; 123: 34; 128: 12; 130: 33; 135: 14; 143: 25. The other uses in the narration are on pp. 23: 7; 112: 12.

49. The one exception, the Vidame's statement, «je me conduisois si mal que la Reine eut *quelque* connoissance de cet attachement,» p. 107: 7-9, actually simply reverses the situation since the speaker is not the observer, but the person observed.

50. *Académie*, s.v. «quelque,» *«Il y a quelque difficulté dans cette affaire,* pour dire, qu'Il y a un peu de difficulté.»

51. Other instances of this usage are found on pp. 32: 31; 39: 26; 54: 4; 54: 23; 69: 18; 74: 25-26; 79: 26; 169: 4. The five other instances of *quelque* as plural adjective are found on pp. 47: 24-25; 92: 29; 98: 30; 165: 19; 170: 7. The first three are of no special interest. The fourth is a case of passing over detail, and the last is a famous illustration of the restraint with which physical effects of passion are treated: «il [Nemours] s'abandonna aux transports de son amour et son cœur en fut tellement pressé qu'il fut contraint de laisser couler *quelques* larmes.»

52. *Mouvement de colère* rather than the essence, *colère. Hardiesse* would seem to describe an infringement of the respect Mme de Clèves feels due her (i.e. injured pride), while *imprudence* obviously alludes to practical rather than sentimental concerns. All this represents the narrator's intervening intellection.

53. The same sort of effect is produced in the narrator's resumé of Mme de Clèves's thought: «Les actions de ce prince s'accordoient trop bien avec ses paroles pour laisser *quelque* doute à cette princesse,» p. 77: 24-26. In M. de Clèves's «vous regretterez *quelque* jour un homme qui vous aimoit d'une passion véritable,» p. 177: 16-17, no sensible difference would be made by the use of *un*. Here the choice of *quelque* brings with it no special nuance.

54. There is another use of *quelque* in the partitive sense, p. 116: 15-16, which carries with it no special emphasis and may be considered typical of court speech patterns.

55. «Le Temps dans *La Princesse de Clèves*,» *Marche Romane*, 9 (1959), 51-58; cf. Francillon, pp. 118-21.

56. On the concept of time in *La Princesse de Clèves*, see Georges Poulet, «Madame de La Fayette,» *Etudes sur le temps humain* (Paris: Plon, 1950), pp. 122-32;

Serge Doubrovsky, «*La Princesse de Clèves*: Une interprétation existentielle,» *La Table Ronde*, 138 (1959), 50; Niderst, pp. 33, 186, et passim; Jean Onimus, «L'Expression du temps dans le roman contemporain,» *Revue de Littérature Comparée*, 28 (1954), 300-01.

57. *Chose* appears approximately one hundred and seventeen times (in addition to the thirty-one occurrences in *quelque chose*), and *passion* approximately one hundred and thirteen times. *Passion* will be discussed in Chapter III.

58. See Harry Ashton, *Madame de La Fayette: sa vie et ses œuvres* (Cambridge: Cambridge University Press, 1922), pp. 80-81, 173; Dédéyan, pp. 74, 77, 147; Haig, pp. 45, 72.

59. Jean de Bazin, *Index de Vocabulaire: La Princesse de Montpensier, La Comtesse de Tende* (Paris: Nizet, 1970), *Montpensier*, p. 22, *Tende*, p. 18. In comparison, the most frequently used nouns in La Rochefoucauld's *Maximes* are, in order of descending occurrence, *homme, esprit, amour, chose, gens, passion*. In Segrais's «Floridon,» they are *amour, temps, vie, esprit, parole, passion, cœur, peur, amitié, chose*. In relation to all words, *chose* is 22nd in frequency in *La Princesse de Clèves*, *passion* 26th, and *amour* 74th. In *Montpensier, passion* is 22nd, *chose* 24th and *amour* 32nd. In *Tende, passion* is 20th, *amour* 57th, *chose* 91st. In the *Maximes, chose* is 16th and *passion* 21st, preceded by *homme* 9th, *esprit* 12th, and *amour* 15th. In «Floridon,» *amour* is 19th, *passion* 35th and *chose* 42nd. This information is taken from Jean de Bazin, *Qui a écrit «la Princesse de Clèves»? Etude de l'attribution de «La Princesse de Clèves» par des moyens de statistique du vocabulaire* (Paris: Nizet, [1971]), pp. 80-81.

60. Not discussed here, because they present no particular anomalies, are the fixed expressions *belles choses*, p. 7: 15-16, *peu de chose*, pp. 53: 21, 153: 11, and *autre chose*, pp. 20: 20, 98: 13-14, 199: 2-3.

61. For example: «Si Mme la Dauphine l' [Mme de Clèves], eût regardée avec attention, elle eust aisément remarqué que les *choses* qu'elle venoit de dire ne luy estoient pas indifférentes,» p. 73: 15-18. In this connection, see section 3 above.

62. *Académie*, s.v. «chose,» «Il se dit indifféremment de tout; sa signification se determinant par la matiere dont on traite.»

63. There are, of course, instances where the progressive substitution of one substantive for another does more than provide variety. For example, after the *aveu*, in the presentation of the heroine's thoughts, her action is referred to serially as «ce qu'elle venoit de faire,» «une chose si hazardeuse,» and «ce remède,» p. 129: 7, 12-13, 17. The development of her thought can be traced through this progression.

64. See also pp. 45: 10-11; 45: 18; 99: 13-14; 137: 6; 160: 23; 172: 25-26; 186: 19; 196: 34. Two of the four uses of the plural *les mêmes choses* fit this category, pp. 145: 34-35; 149: 11-12. The other uses of *les mêmes choses* serve different ends. In one case, the expression is modified by *à peu près* and is the transition from a presentation of the Prince's interiority to one of his wife's thoughts, p. 145: 23. In the other, the adjective is actualized by context: «elle [Mme de Clèves] entra avec un esprit ouvert et tranquille *dans les mesmes choses* qu'elle sembloit d'abord ne daigner pas entendre,» p. 115: 17-19.

65. Pages 26: 23; 29: 9; 44: 3-4; 47: 7-8; 48: 8-9; 49: 21; 50: 6-7; 52: 15-16; 58: 7-8; 74: 18-19; 76: 11; 76: 22; 82: 7; 102: 2; 109: 26; 117: 21-22; 133: 6; 138: 17; 147: 5-6; 157: 34; 181: 3-4; 201: 5-6. The reverse is true of the indefinite, as opposed to definite, plural on pp. 128: 19-20.

66. Pages 47: 7-8; 50: 6-7; 52: 15-16; 82: 7; 147: 5-6; 157: 34; 181: 3-4.

67. Not discussed here are: «Mme de Chartres n'avoit pas voulu laisser voir à sa fille qu'elle connaissoit ses sentimens pour ce prince, de peur de se rendre suspecte sur les *choses* qu'elle avoit envie de luy dire,» p. 52: 13-16; «la connoissance qu'ils avoient de leurs sentimens leur donnoit une aigreur qui paroissoit en toutes *choses*,» p. 82: 5-7; «c'estoit une *chose* où elle avoit esté préférée à plusieurs autres princesses,» p. 147: 5-6; «Quoy que ce fût une *chose* facheuse pour M. de Clèves de ne pas conduire Mme Elizabeth,» p. 157: 34-35.

68. E.g. Antoine Adam, *Histoire de la littérature française au XVIIe siècle* (Paris: del Duca, 1958), IV, 193.

69. On this point, Valincour, pp. 255-56, notes the proliferation of subordinate clauses introduced by *que*. Tiefenbrun, «The Art,» pp. 41-42, discusses the ways in which such sentences can convey the concept of dissimulation, the chain of court gossip, or produce effects of repetition. Fabre, *L'Art de l'analyse*, p. 49, notes that Mme de Lafayette's syntax is light in comparison to that of her predecessors and points out that the semi-Latin construction illustrates her mode of thought. Further interpretations of this element of Mme de Lafayette's style may be found in Woshinsky, pp. 82, 87; Niderst, pp. 164, 179, et passim.

70. «The action of setting forth in words by mentioning recognizable features or characteristic marks; verbal representation or portraiture,» *OED*, s.v. «description.»

71. «A figure of speech, whereby the supposed words or actions of another are imitated,» *OED*, s.v. «mimesis.»

72. Tiefenbrun is perhaps the only student of the novel who consciously treats *mimesis* and not description. Cf. Part I, Chapter II above, on the concept of secondary mimesis.

73. «La Princesse de Clèves,» *Nouvelle Revue Française*, 48 (1937), 514.


# CHAPTER III


1. The three uses of *passionné*, pp. 27: 13; 46: 10-11; 175: 3-7, also contribute to the effect of thematic repetition. The present discussion is limited to the substantives *passion, amour, inclination* and *sentiment*, the verb *aimer* and the adjective *amoureux*. For an extensive analysis of much of the language of gallantry in the seventeenth century, see Bernard Quemada, «Le 'Commerce amoureux' dans les romans mondains (1640-1700): Etude sur le vocabulaire de la galanterie au XVIIe siècle,» Diss. Faculté des Lettres, Paris, 1949.

2. Furetière, «*Passion*, en Morale, se dit des differentes agitations de l'ame selon les divers objets qui se presentent à ses sens . . . se dit par excellence de l'amour.» The definitions in *Académie*, s.v. «pâtir,» are similar.

3. This is made explicit near the end of Part III: «elle demeura chez elle, peu occupée du grand changement qui se préparoit,» p. 154: 11-12.

4. In three cases, pp. 73: 35-74: 2; 75: 18-20; 164: 29-30, the use offers no special nuance. The sixth occurrence, p. 55: 25, is discussed below.

5. See Quemada, pp. 311-12, who says that this usage of *passion* is found only in the works of writers of very high society.

6. Fifty-one of the one hundred and thirteen uses, or forty-five percent, are in direct discourse. The general distribution differs little from that of *chose* or from the proportion of direct discourse in the novel. The pattern of distribution here provides a fairly good outline of the novél's structure. In Part I, the noun is used twenty-five times, of which six are found in the «digressions,» two in plot-advancing direct discourse, and seventeen in narration (including indirect discourse and interiority). In Part II, *passion* occurs twenty-six times: twelve times in the «digressions,» six times in plot-advancing direct discourse, and eight times in the narration. Part III contains twenty-one uses of *passion*, one in a «digression,» nine in direct discourse, and eleven in the narration. Part IV has forty uses of *passion*, none in «digressions,» fifteen in direct discourse, and twenty-five in the narration. Even without eliminating from direct discourse and narration those usages which do not relate to the principals, the progression is clear.

7. The noun *aigreur* is used eleven times, the adjective *aigre* once and the verb *aigrir* twice. Dubois gives *violence* and *colère, irritation*. The noun is used in both senses in *La Princesse de Clèves*, and, with one possible exception, p. 13: 10-11, is always associated with jealousy: pp. 54: 4; 82: 7; 97: 1-2 (cited by Dubois as an example of the substantive used in the sense of *violence*); 108: 26; 112: 20; 113: 34; 120: 7; 120: 11; 120: 16; 155: 14. The adjective *aigre* is also used in this context, p. 45: 4-5, as are two of the four occurrences of the verb *aigrir*, pp. 64: 19; 112: 17. The association is attested by Littré, s.v. «aigreur,» who cites Corneille, *Pompée*, V, 2: «L'impérieuse aigreur de l'âpre jalousie.»

8. On the progression *intérêt, inclination, passion* in reference to the heroine, see below the discussion of *inclination*, and Burkart, p. 161.

9. The same matter-of-fact pattern continues until the end of the novel; pp. 181: 13; 184: 8-10; 199: 28. In the description of Mme de Clèves's agitation following her interview with Nemours, *passion* appears in a diminished sense, as one of a number of emotions: «Elle fut étonnée de ce qu'elle avoit fait; elle s'en repentit; elle en eut de la joye: tous ses sentimens estoient pleins de trouble et de *passion*,» p. 196: 18-21.

10. The noun appears twenty-five times in Part I. Six of these are in digressions. Of the nineteen remaining usages, eight refer to the Prince's sentiments.

11. *Amoureux* is always used as an adjective, not a substantive, although that usage was also possible; Furetière, s.v. «amoureux,» and *Académie*, s.v. «aimer.»

12. According to Bazin's figures, those verbs used more often than *aimer* are, in order of frequency, *être, avoir, faire, voir, pouvoir, donner, trouver, venir, aller* and *savoir*.

13. Fifty-one instances, of which ten are in the locution *pour l'amour de*, reducing the effective occurrence to forty-one. On the locution, see Dubois and Littré, s.v. «amour.» The substantive is always singular and never used to designate the love-object rather than the emotion. The existence of these possibilities is attested in *Académie*, s.v. «aimer,» and Furetière, s.v. «amour.» On the use of the plural, see Quemada, p. 305, who remarks its decreased usage as compared to the period before 1640.

14. While Furetière says that *inclination* «se dit aussi de l'amour, de la bonne

volonté qu'on a pour quelqu'un,» it is impossible that the notion of naturalness contained in *inclination*'s wider meaning not add this connotation when the noun is used in the sense of love. Cf. also *Académie*, s.v. «déclin.»

15. Pages 88: 31; 89: 3; 97: 27; 98: 6; 121: 21 (in soliloquy); 177: 31-32; 184: 4; 194: 12-13. The noun appears a total of thirty-two times. Its uses to refer to Mme de Clèves's feelings for Nemours represent the largest single category.

16. Cf. Tiefenbrun, pp. 31-32, for an analysis of the use of *amour, passion* and *inclination*, which differs from the foregoing in both method and results.

# SELECTED BIBLIOGRAPHY

Adam, Antoine. *Histoire de la littérature française au XVII$^e$ siècle*. 5 vols. Paris: del Duca, 1958.

———, ed. *Les Romanciers du XVII$^e$ siècle: Sorel, Scarron, Furetière, Mme de La Fayette*. Paris: Gallimard, 1958.

Alciatore, Jules C. «Stendhal et *La Princesse de Clèves*.» *Stendhal-Club*, 1 (1959), 281-94.

Allentuch, Harriet R. «Pauline and the Princesse de Clèves.» *Modern Language Quarterly*, 30 (1969), 171-82.

Ames, Van Meter. *Aesthetics of the Novel*. 1928; rpt. New York: Gordian Press, 1966.

Arland, Marcel. «Quelques Etapes de l'évolution du roman au XVII$^e$ siècle.» *Le Préclassicisme français*. Ed. Jean Tortel. Paris: Les Cahiers du Sud, 1952, pp. 196-207.

———. «Mme de La Fayette et la *Princesse de Clèves*.» *Les Echanges*. Paris: Gallimard, 1946, pp. 81-105.

Ashton, Harry. «L'Anonymat des œuvres de Mme de La Fayette.» *Revue d'Histoire Littéraire de la France*, 21 (1914), 712-15.

———. «Essai de bibliographie des œuvres de Mme de La Fayette.» *Revue d'Histoire Littéraire de la France*, 20 (1913), 899-918.

———. *Mme de La Fayette: sa vie et ses œuvres*. Cambridge: Cambridge University Press, 1922.

Auerbach, Erich. «'La Cour et la ville.'» *Scenes from the Drama of European Literature: Six Essays*. 1959; rpt. Gloucester, Mass.: Smith, 1973, pp. 133-79.

———. *Mimesis, the Representation of Reality in Western Literature*. Trans. Willard Trask. Princeton: Princeton University Press, 1953.

Baldensperger, Fernand. «A propos de 'l'aveu' de la *Princesse de Clèves*.» *Revue de Philologie Française et de Littérature*, 15 (1901), 26-31.

Baldner, Ralph W. «Aspects of the Nouvelle in France Between 1600 and 1660.» *Modern Language Quarterly*, 22 (1961), 351-56.

———. «Eloquence in the Seventeenth-Century French Novel.» *Romance Notes*, 6 (1964), 55-56.

Bally, Charles. «Figures de pensée et formes linguistiques.» *Germanisch-Romanische Monatsschrift*, 6 (1914), 405-22, 456-70.

———. «Le Style indirect libre en français moderne.» *Germanisch-Romanische Monatsschrift*, 4 (1912), 549-56, 597-606.

———. *Traité de stylistique française*. 3rd ed. 2 vols. Paris: Klincksieck, and Geneva: Georg, 1951.

Bar, Francis. «Le Roman réaliste en France au XVIIᵉ siècle.» *Stil- und Formprobleme in der Literatur*. Heidelberg: Winter-Universitätsverlag, 1959, pp. 215-23.

Barnwell, Henry T. «Mme de La Fayette. Extract from *La Princesse de Clèves*.» *The Art of Criticism: Essays in French Literary Analysis*. Ed. Peter H. Nurse. Edinburgh: Edinburgh University Press, 1969, pp. 113-27.

Bart, Benjamin F. «Aesthetic Distance in *Madame Bovary*.» *PMLA*, 69 (1954), 1112-26.

Barthes, Roland. *Le Degré zéro de l'écriture. Eléments de sémiologie*. Paris: Gonthier, 1964.

———. «L'Effet de réel.» *Communications*, 11 (1968), 84-89.

———. *Essais critiques*. Paris: Seuil, 1964.

———. «Introduction à l'analyse structurale des récits.» *Communications*, 8 (1966), 1-27.

Bazin, Jean de. *Index de vocabulaire: La Princesse de Montpensier, La Comtesse de Tende*. Paris: Nizet, 1970.

———. *Index du vocabulaire de La Princesse de Clèves*. Paris: Nizet, 1967.

———. *Index du vocabulaire des Maximes de La Rochefoucauld*. Paris: Nizet, 1967.

———. *Lettres de Mme de Lafayette au chevalier de Lescheraine, Texte provenant des Archives du Turin*. Paris: Nizet, 1970.

———. *Qui a écrit «la Princesse de Clèves»? Etude de l'attribution de «la Princesse de Clèves» par des moyens de statistique du vocabulaire*. Paris: Nizet, [1971].

Bénichou, Paul. *Morales du grand siècle*. Paris: Gallimard, 1948.

Benveniste, Emile. *Problèmes de linguistique générale*. Paris: Gallimard, 1966.

Bergevin, Annette de. «Le Repos de Mme de Clèves.» *Esprit*, 31 (1963),

662-64.

*Bibliothèque Universelle des Romans, ouvrage périodique.* January 1776.

Bonnet, Henri. *Roman et poésie: Essai sur l'esthétique des genres.* Paris: Nizet, 1951.

Booth, Wayne C. *The Rhetoric of Fiction.* Chicago: University of Chicago Press, 1961.

Borgerhoff, E.B.O. *The Freedom of French Classicism.* Princeton: Princeton University Press, 1950.

Bouhours, Dominique. *Doutes sur la langue françoise.* Nouvelle édition. Paris: Bénard, 1691.

Bounoure, Gabriel. «Les Mille Oiseaux du silence, II. La perle blanche.» *Mercure de France,* 352 (1964), 426-35.

Brantôme, Pierre. *Les Dames galantes.* Ed. Maurice Rat. Paris: Garnier, 1947.

Bray, Bernard. *L'Art de la lettre amoureuse: Des manuels aux romans (1550-1700).* Paris and The Hague: Mouton, 1967.

Bray, René. *La Préciosité et les précieux.* Paris: Nizet, n.d.

Bremond, Claude. «La Logique des possibles narratifs.» *Communications,* 8 (1966), 60-76.

―――. «Le Message narratif.» *Communications,* 4 (1964), 4-32.

Brody, Jules. «*La Princesse de Clèves* and the Myth of Courtly Love.» *University of Toronto Quarterly,* 38 (1969), 105-35.

Brown, Huntington. *Prose Styles: Five Primary Types.* Minneapolis: University of Minnesota Press, 1966.

Brunot, Ferdinand. *Histoire de la langue française des origines à 1900.* 9 vols. Paris: Colin, 1930.

―――, and Charles Bruneau. *Précis de grammaire historique de la langue française.* Paris: Masson, 1933.

Burkart, Rosemarie. *Die Kunst des Masses in Mme de Lafayette's «Princesse de Clèves.»* Bonn and Köln: Röhrscheid, 1933.

Butor, Michel. «Sur 'La Princesse de Clèves.'» *Répertoire.* Paris: Editions de Minuit, 1960, pp. 74-78.

Cahen, Jacques-Gabriel. *Le Vocabulaire de Racine.* 1946; rpt. Geneva: Slatkine Reprints, 1970.

Camus, Albert. «L'Intelligence et l'échafaud.» *Problèmes du roman,* numéro spécial de la revue *Confluences.* Ed. Jean Prévost. Lyons, 1943, pp. 218-23.

Carré, Marie-Rose. «La Rencontre inachevée: Etude sur la structure de *La Princesse de Clèves.*» *PMLA,* 87 (1972), 475-82.

Cayrou, Gaston. *Le Français classique.* Paris: Didier, 1948.

Chaillet, Jean. «Etude stylistique. *La Princesse de Clèves.*» *Information*

*Littéraire*, 19 (1967), 132-38.

Chamard, Henri, and Gustave Rudler. «Les Sources historiques de *La Princesse de Clèves*.» *Revue du Seizième Siècle*, 2 (1914), 92-131.

———. «Les Sources historiques de *La Princesse de Clèves*: les épisodes historiques.» *Revue du Seizième Siècle*, 2 (1914), 289-321.

———. «La Couleur historique dans *La Princesse de Clèves*.» *Revue du Seizième Siècle*, 5 (1917-18), 1-20.

———. «L'Histoire et la fiction dans *La Princesse de Clèves*.» *Revue du Seizième Siècle*, 5 (1917-18), 231-43.

Chardonne, Jacques. «La Princesse de Clèves.» *Nouvelle Revue Française*, 48 (1937), 513-15.

[Charnes, Jean-Antoine de]. *Conversations sur la critique de La princesse de Clèves*. Paris: Barbin, 1679.

Chatman, Seymour. «New Ways of Analyzing Narrative Structure with an Example from Joyce's *Dubliners*.» *Language and Style*, 2.1 (1969), 3-36.

———, ed. *Literary Style: A Symposium*. Trans. (in part) Seymour Chatman. London and New York: Oxford University Press, 1971.

———, and Samuel Levin, eds. *Essays on the Language of Literature*. Boston: Houghton Mifflin, 1967.

Cioranescu, Alexandre. «La Nouvelle française et la 'comedia' espagnole au XVIIe siècle.» *CAIEF*, 18 (1966), 79-87.

Cohen, Jean. *Structure du langage poétique*. Paris: Flammarion, 1966.

Cohen, Marcel. «Le Style indirect libre et l'imparfait en français après 1850.» *Europe*, 30.77 (1952), 62-69.

*The Compact Edition of the Oxford English Dictionary*. 2 vols. Glasgow and New York: Oxford University Press, 1971.

Coulet, Henri. *Le Roman jusqu'à la Révolution*. 2 vols. Paris: Colin, 1967-68.

Cressot, Marcel. *Le Style et ses techniques: Précis d'analyse stylistique*. 3rd ed. Paris: Presses Universitaires de France, 1956.

Croce, Benedetto. «La Princesse de Clèves.» *Quaderni della critica*, 7 (1951), 144-46.

Daiches, David. *A Study of Literature for Readers and Critics*. Ithaca, New York: Cornell University Press, 1943.

Daix, Pierre. *Nouvelle critique et art moderne, essai*. Paris: Seuil, 1968.

Dallas, Dorothy. *Le Roman français de 1660 à 1680*. Paris: Gamber, 1932.

D'A[storg], B[ertrand]. «La Princesse de Clèves.» *Esprit*, 32 (1964), 541.

D'Astorg, Bertrand. «Le Refus de Madame de Clèves.» *Esprit*, 31 (1963), 654-62.

Dédéyan, Charles. *Madame de Lafayette*. Paris: Société d'Edition d'Enseignement Supérieur, 1955.

De Jongh, William. «La Rochefoucauld et *La Princesse de Clèves*.» *Symposium*, 13 (1959), 271-77.

Delbouille, Paul. «Réflexions sur l'état présent de la stylistique littéraire.» *Cahiers d'Analyse Textuelle*, 6 (1964), 7-22.

Delhez-Sarlet, Claudette. «Une Page de *La Princesse de Clèves*.» *Cahiers d'Analyse Textuelle*, 3 (1961), 54-66.

———. «Style indirect libre et 'point de vue' dans *La Princesse de Clèves*.» *Cahiers d'Analyse Textuelle*, 6 (1964), 70-80.

Delpech, Jeanine. «La Princesse de Clèves.» *Les Nouvelles Littéraires*, 1614 (7 August 1958), 1-2.

Derche, Roland. «La Princesse de Clèves.» *Etudes de textes français*. Nouvelle série III, XVIIᵉ siècle. Paris: Société d'Edition d'Enseignement Supérieur, 1965, pp. 327-50.

De Rosa, Renato T. *Il Preziosismo di Madame de La Fayette: Aspetti e Richerche*. Naples: Istituto editoriale del mezzogiorno, 1969.

Descartes, René. *Les Passions de l'âme*. Paris: Gallimard, 1953.

*Dictionnaire de l'Académie françoise*. 2 vols. Paris: Coignard, 1694.

Doležel, Lubomír. «Vers la stylistique structurale.» *Travaux Linguistiques de Prague*, 1 (1964), 257-66.

Doubrovsky, Serge. «*La Princesse de Clèves*: une interprétation existentielle.» *La Table Ronde*, 138 (1959), 36-51.

Dubois, Jean, René Lagane, and Alain Lerond. *Dictionnaire du français classique*. Paris: Larousse, 1971.

Dubois, Jean, *et al. Rhétorique générale*. Paris: Larousse, 1970.

Ducrot, Oswald, *et al. Qu'est-ce que le structuralisme?* Paris: Seuil, 1968.

Du Marsais, César Chesnau. *Des Tropes ou des différens sens dans lesquels on peut prendre un même mot dans une même langue*. 3rd ed. Paris: Prault, 1775.

[Du Plaisir]. *Sentimens sur les lettres, et sur l'histoire, avec des scrupules sur le stile*. Paris: Blageart, 1683.

Dupriez, Bernard. *L'Etude des styles, ou la communication en littérature*. Paris: Didier, 1969.

Durry, Marie-Jeanne. *Madame de la Fayette*. Paris: Mercure de France, 1962.

———. «Madame de La Fayette.» *Mercure de France*, 340 (1960), 193-217.

———. «Le Monologue intérieur dans *La Princesse de Clèves*.» *La Littérature narrative d'imagination, des genres littéraires aux techniques d'expression*. Paris: Presses Universitaires de France, 1959, pp. 86-93.

Enkvist, Nils E., Michael Gregory, and John Spencer. *Linguistics and Style*. Oxford: Oxford University Press, 1964.

Fabre, Jean. *L'Art de l'analyse dans la Princesse de Clèves*. Paris: Ophrys, 1970.

———. «Bienséance et sentiment chez Madame de Lafayette.» *CAIEF*, 11 (1959), 33-66.

Flaubert, Gustave. *Oeuvres complètes*. Eds. Jean Bruneau and Bernard Masson. 2 vols. Paris: Seuil, 1964.

Forster, Edward M. *Aspects of the Novel*. 1927; rpt. London: Arnold, 1961.

Fougères, Michel. *La «Liebestod» dans le roman français, anglais et allemand au XVIIIe siècle*. Ottawa: Naaman, 1974.

Fowler, Roger, ed. *Essays on Style and Language: Linguistic and Critical Approaches to Literary Style*. New York: The Humanities Press, 1966.

Fraisse, Simone. «Le 'Repos' de Mme de Clèves.» *Esprit*, 11 (1961), 56-67.

France, Anatole. «Mme de La Fayette.» *La Vie littéraire*. 4th series. Paris: Calmann Lévy, 1892, pp. 291-99.

France, Peter. *Racine's Rhetoric*. Oxford: Clarendon Press, 1965.

Francillon, Roger. *L'Oeuvre romanesque de Madame de La Fayette*. Paris: Corti, 1973.

Freeman, Donald C., ed. *Linguistics and Literary Style*. New York: Holt, Rinehart and Winston, 1970.

Friedrich, Klaus. «Mme de Lafayette in der Forschung (1950-65).» *Romanistisches Jahrbuch*, 17 (1966), 112-49.

———. «Eine Theorie des 'Roman nouveau.'» *Romanistisches Jahrbuch*, 14 (1963), 118-32.

Froment-Maurice, Henri. «La Princesse de Clèves.» *Esprit*, 306 (1962), 877-79.

Furetière, Antoine. *Dictionnaire universel contenant généralement tous les mots françois tant vieux que modernes*. Nouvelle édition corrigée et augmentée. 2 vols. The Hague and Rotterdam: Leers, 1694.

Galet, Yvette. *L'Evolution de l'ordre des mots dans la phrase française de 1600 à 1700*. Paris: Presses Universitaires de France, 1971.

———. «Illustration de la théorie des niveaux d'énonciation.» *Langue Française*, 21 (1974), 26-42.

Galey, Matthieu. «Mme de La Fayette.» *Cahiers des Saisons*, 12.47 (1966), 135-50.

Genette, Gérard. *Figures III*. Paris: Seuil, 1972.

———. «Frontières du récit.» *Communications*, 8 (1966), 152-63.

———. «Vraisemblance et motivation.» *Communications*, 11 (1968), 5-21.

Gilbert, Pierre. «A propos de *la Princesse de Clèves*. La comédie et le roman.» *Revue Critique des Idées et des Livres*, 2 (1908), 102-17.

Girard, René. *Mensonge romantique et vérité romanesque*. Paris: Grasset, 1961.

Godenne, René. «L'Association 'nouvelle-petit roman' entre 1650 et 1750.» *CAIEF*, 18 (1966), 67-78.

Goldman, Lucien. *Pour une sociologie du roman*. Paris: Gallimard, 1964.

Goode, William O. «A Mother's Goals in *La Princesse de Clèves*: Worldly and Spiritual Distinction.» *Neophilologus*, 56 (1972), 398-406.

Gougenheim, Georges. «La Présentation du discours direct dans *La Princesse de Clèves* et dans *Dominique*.» *Le Français Moderne*, 6.4 (1938), 305-20.

Green, Frederick C. *French Novelists, Manners and Ideas from the Renaissance to the Revolution*. New York: Ungar, 1964.

———. «Some Observations on Technique and Form in the French Seventeenth and Eighteenth Century Novel.» *Stil- und Formprobleme in der Literatur*. Heidelberg: Winter-Universitätsverlag, 1959, pp. 208-15.

Greimas, A.J. *Du Sens: essais sémiotiques*. Paris: Seuil, 1970.

———. «La Structure des actants du récit: Essai d'approche générative.» *Word*, 23 (1967), 221-38.

———. «Structure et histoire.» *Les Temps Modernes*, 246 (1966), 815-27.

Grossvogel, David I. «*La Princesse de Clèves*.» *Limits of the Novel*. Ithaca, New York: Cornell University Press, 1968, pp. 108-35.

Haig, Stirling. «La Rochefoucauld's *Mémoires* and an Episode of *La Princesse de Clèves*.» *Studi Francesi*, 36 (1968), 477-79.

———. *Madame de Lafayette*. New York: Twayne Publishers, 1970.

Haillant, Marguerite. «*La Princesse de Clèves*: Une scène de jalousie.» *Information Littéraire*, 26 (1974), 134-38.

Hall, Douglas R. «A Structural Analysis of the Fictional Works of Madame de La Fayette.» Diss. University of Maryland, 1968.

Hartle, Robert W. «Racine's Hidden Metaphors.» *Modern Language Notes*, 76 (1961), 132-39.

Haussonville, le Comte de. *Madame de La Fayette*. 4th ed. Paris: Hachette, 1919.

Henriot, Emile. «Mme de La Fayette et la *Princesse de Clèves*.» *Le Temps*, 28299 (7 March 1939), 3.

———. «Mme de La Fayette et 'le Triomphe de l'indifférence.'» *Le Temps*, 27806 (26 October 1937), 3.

Henry, Albert. «L'Expressivité du dialogue dans le roman.» *La Littérature narrative d'imagination, des genres littéraires aux techniques d'expression*. Paris: Presses Universitaires de France, 1961, pp. 3-19.

Hipp, Marie-Thérèse. «Le Mythe de Tristan et Iseut et *La Princesse de Clèves*.» *Revue d'Histoire Littéraire de la France*, 65 (1965), 398-414.

Hoog, Armand. «Sacrifice d'une Princesse.» *La Nef*, 6.55 (1949), 16-25.

Huet, Pierre D. *Lettre de Monsieur Huet à Monsieur de Segrais: De l'origine des romans*, in *Oeuvres complètes de Mesdames de La Fayette, de Tencin et de Fontaines*. Eds. Etienne and Antoine Jay. Paris: Moutardier, 1832, I, 1-74.

Humphrey, Robert. *Stream of Consciousness in the Modern Novel*. Berkeley, Los Angeles, and London: University of California Press, 1954.

Iser, Wolfgang. *The Implied Reader: Patterns of Communication in Prose Fiction from Bunyan to Beckett*. Baltimore and London: Johns Hopkins University Press, 1974.

Jakobson, Roman. *Essais de linguistique générale*. Trans. Nicolas Ruwet. Paris: Editions de Minuit, 1963.

James, Henry. *The Art of the Novel: Critical Prefaces*. New York and London: Scribner's, 1934.

Jay, Etienne, and Antoine Jay, eds. *Oeuvres complètes de Mesdames de La Fayette, de Tencin et de Fontaines*. Paris: Moutardier, 1825, vols. 1-3.

Jennings, L. Chantal. «L'Amour-passion de Tristan à l'œuvre proustienne: vicissitudes d'un mythe.» *Symposium*, 25 (1971), 123-38.

Jones, Shirley. «Examples of Sensibility in the Late Seventeenth-Century Feminine Novel in France.» *Modern Language Review*, 61 (1966), 199-208.

Joran, Théodore. «*La Princesse de Clèves.*» *Les Féministes avant le féminisme*. 2nd series. Paris: Beauchesne, 1935, pp. 82-107.

Josipovici, Gabriel. *The World and the Book: A Study of Modern Fiction*. Stanford: Stanford University Press, 1971.

Judrin, Roger. «La Rochefoucauld et Mme de La Fayette.» *Nouvelle Revue Française*, 15 (1967), 1224-29.

Kaps, Helen K. *Moral Perspective in «La Princesse de Clèves.»* Eugene, Oregon: University of Oregon Books, 1968.

Kassaï, Georges. «L'Indirect dans la 'Princesse de Clèves.'» *Lettres Nouvelles*, (1970), 123-32.

Köhler, Erich. *Madame de Lafayettes «La Princesse de Clèves»: Studien zur Form des klassischen Romans*. Hamburg: Cram, de Gruyter and Co., 1959.

Krömer, Wolfram. «Novellistik und 'nouveau roman' des französischen 17. Jahrhunderts.» *Zeitschrift für Französische Sprache und Literatur*, 80 (1970), 230-57.

La Fayette, Marie-Madeleine de. *Correspondance*. Eds. André Beaunier and [Georges Roth]. 2 vols. Paris: Gallimard, 1942.

———. *Histoire de Mme Henriette d'Angleterre, suivie de Mémoires de la cour de France pour les années 1688 et 1689*. Ed. Gilbert Sigaux. Paris:

Mercure de France, 1965.

[Lafayette, Marie-Madeleine de]. *La Princesse de Clèves*. 4 vols. in 2. Paris: Barbin, 1678.

Lafayette, Marie-Madeleine de. *La Princesse de Clèves*. Ed. Emile Magne. Geneva: Droz, and Lille: Giard, 1950.

———. *La Princesse de Clèves, La Princesse de Montpensier*. Ed. Gilbert Sigaux. Paris: Colin, 1960.

———. *La Princesse de Clèves*. Ed. Peter H. Nurse. London: Harrap, 1971.

———. *Romans et nouvelles*. Ed. Emile Magne. Paris: Garnier, 1961.

———. *Vie de la Princesse d'Angleterre*. Ed. Marie-Thérèse Hipp. Geneva: Droz, 1967.

Lanfredini, Dina. «L'Originalità della *Princesse de Montpensier* di Mme de La Fayette.» *Rivista di Letterature Moderne e Comparate*, 13 (1960), 61-88.

Lapointe, René. «La Princesse de Clèves par elle-même.» *Travaux de Linguistique et de Littérature, publiés par le Centre de Philologie et de Littérature de l'Université de Strasbourg*, 4.2 (1966), 51-58.

Laudy, Bernard. «La Vision tragique de Madame de La Fayette, ou un jansénisme athée.» *Revue de l'Institut de Sociologie de l'Université Libre de Bruxelles*, 3 (1969), 449-62.

Laugaa, Maurice. *Lectures de Mme de Lafayette*. Paris: Colin, 1971.

Lawrence, Francis W. «*La Princesse de Clèves* Reconsidered.» *French Review*, 39 (1965), 15-21.

Lebeau, Jean. «De la *Modification* de Michel Butor à la *Princesse de Clèves*.» *Cahiers du Sud*, 51 (1964), 285-91.

Lebois, André. «Blonde et folle Princesse de Clèves.» *XVIIe Siècle, recherches et portraits*. Paris: Denoël, 1966, pp. 291-309.

Le Hir, Yves. *Analyses stylistiques*. Paris: Colin, 1965.

Léo, Maurice. «La Rhétorique de l'obstacle surmonté chez Corneille et chez Madame de La Fayette.» *Missions et démarches de la critique. Mélanges offerts au professeur Jacques Vier*. Paris: Klincksieck, 1973, pp. 719-31.

Leov, Nola M. «Sincerity and Order in the *Princesse de Clèves*.» *AUMLA*, 30 (1968), 133-50.

Lips, Marguerite. *Le Style indirect libre*. Paris: Payot, 1926.

Littré, Emile. *Dictionnaire de la langue française*. Edition intégrale. 7 vols. Paris: Gallimard-Hachette, 1970.

Lodge, David. *The Novelist at the Crossroads and Other Essays on Fiction and Criticism*. Ithaca, New York: Cornell University Press, 1971.

Lotringer, Sylvère. «Le Roman impossible.» *Poétique*, 1.3 (1970), 297-321.

———. «La Structuration romanesque.» *Critique*, 277 (1970), 498-529.

Lukás, Georg. *The Historical Novel*. Trans. Hannah and Stanley Mitchell. Boston: Beacon Press, 1963.

Macherey, Pierre. «L'Analyse littéraire, tombeau des structures.» *Les Temps Modernes*, 246 (1966), 907-28.

Magendie, Maurice. *Du Nouveau sur l'Astrée*. Paris: Champion, 1927.

———. *La Politesse mondaine et les théories de l'honnêteté en France au XVIIe siècle de 1600 à 1660*. 1925; rpt. Geneva: Slatkine Reprints, 1970.

———. *Le Roman français au XVIIe siècle de l'«Astrée» au «Grand Cyrus.»* 1932; rpt. Geneva: Slatkine Reprints, 1970.

Magny, Claude-Edmonde. *Histoire du roman français depuis 1918*. 2 vols. Paris: Seuil, 1950.

Malraux, André. *La Condition humaine*. Ed. revue et corrigée. Paris: Gallimard, 1946.

———. *Les Conquérants*. Paris: Grasset, 1928.

Marouzeau, Jules. *Précis de stylistique française*. Paris: Masson, 1969.

Martin, George W. «Constants in the Fiction of Mme de La Fayette.» *Annali. Istituto universitario orientale, Napoli, Sezione romanza*, 14 (1972), 45-74.

McNeill, Isabelle F.E. «L'Univers dramatique de Mme de La Fayette.» Diss. Stanford, 1970.

Ménage, Gilles. *Ménagiana ou les Bons Mots et Remarques critiques de Monsieur de Ménage, recueillies par ses amis*. 3rd ed. 4 vols. Paris: Delaulne, 1715.

[Ménage, Gilles]. *Observations de Monsieur de Ménage sur la langue françoise*. Paris: Barbin, 1672.

Milic, Louis T. «Unconscious Ordering in the Prose of Swift.» *The Computer and Literary Style, Introductory Essays and Studies*. Ed. Jacob Leed. Kent, Ohio: Kent State University Press, 1966, pp. 79-106.

Mitterand, Henri, and Jacques Petit. «Index et concordances dans l'étude des textes littéraires.» *Cahiers de Lexicologie*, 3 (1961), 160-75.

Moore, Will G. *French Classical Literature: An Essay*. Oxford: Oxford University Press, 1961.

Moréas, Jean. «Mme de La Fayette.» *Vers et Prose*, 15 (1908), 58-69.

Morier, Henri. *La Psychologie des styles*. Geneva: Georg, 1959.

Muller, Marcel. *Les Voix narratives dans la «Recherche du temps perdu.»* Geneva: Droz, 1965.

Nicolich, Robert N. «The Language of Vision in *La Princesse de Clèves*: The Baroque Principle of Control and Release.» *Language and Style*, 4 (1971), 279-96.

Niderst, Alain. *La Princesse de Clèves, le roman paradoxal.* Paris: Larousse, 1973.

Nurse, Peter H. *Classical Voices: Studies of Corneille, Racine, Molière, Mme de Lafayette.* London: Harrap, 1971.

Onimus, Jean. «L'Expression du temps dans le roman contemporain.» *Revue de Littérature Comparée*, 28.3 (1954), 299-317.

Peyre, Henri. *Qu'est-ce que le classicisme?* Edition revue et augmentée. Paris: Nizet, 1965.

Picard, Raymond. *Two Centuries of French Literature.* Trans. John Cairncross. New York and Toronto: McGraw-Hill, 1969-70.

Pingaud, Bernard. *Mme de La Fayette par elle-même.* Paris: Seuil, 1959.

———. «Les Secrets de Mme de La Fayette.» *Pensée Française*, 16.13 (1957), 20-23.

Pizzorusso, Arnoldo. *La Poetica del romanzo in Francia (1660-1685).* Caltanissetta and Rome: Sciascia, 1962.

Pons, Roger. «La Princesse de Clèves.» *Procès de l'amour.* 2nd ed. Paris and Tournai: Casterman, 1957, pp. 39-48.

Pouillon, Jean. «Présentation: un essai de définition.» *Les Temps Modernes*, 246 (1966), 769-90.

Poulet, Georges. «Mme de La Fayette.» *Etudes sur le temps humain.* Paris: Plon, 1950, pp. 122-32.

Preminger, Alex, ed. *Encyclopedia of Poetry and Poetics.* Princeton: Princeton University Press, 1965.

Quemada, Bernard. «Le 'Commerce amoureux' dans les romans mondains (1640-1700). Etude sur le vocabulaire de la galanterie au XVIIe siècle.» Diss. Faculté des Lettres, Paris, 1949.

Racine, Jean. *Oeuvres complètes.* Ed. Raymond Picard. 2 vols. Paris: Gallimard, 1950 and 1960.

Raitt, Janet. *Madame de Lafayette and «La Princesse de Clèves.»* London: Harrap, 1971.

Ramsey, Jerome A. «Valincour and the Critical Tradition.» *Modern Philology*, 65 (1968), 325-33.

Ravoux, Elizabeth. «Sur une page de *De l'amour.* Mme de La Fayette et Stendhal.» *Stendhal-Club*, 14 (1971), 63-68.

Redhead, Ruth W. «Love and Death in the Fictional Works of Madame de Lafayette.» Diss. University of Minnesota, 1971.

Riffaterre, Michael. «Criteria for Style Analysis.» *Word*, 15 (1959), 154-74.

———. *Essais de stylistique structurale.* Paris: Flammarion, 1971.

———. «Stylistic Context.» *Word*, 16 (1960), 207-18.

Robert, Paul. *Dictionnaire alphabétique et analogique de la langue françai-*

*se*. 6 vols. Paris: Société du Nouveau Littré, 1966.

Rosso, Corrado. *Il Serpente e la sirena: Dalla paura del dolore alla paura della felicità*. Naples: Edizioni Scientifiche Italiane, 1972, pp. 207-17.

Rougemont, Denis de. *Love in the Western World*. Trans. Montgomery Belgion. Revised and augmented ed. Greenwich, Connecticut: Fawcett Publications, 1966.

Rousset, Jean. «Echanges obliques et 'paroles obscures' dans *La Princesse de Clèves*.» *Littérature, Histoire, Linguistique: Recueil d'études offert à Bernard Gagnebin*. Lausanne: L'Age d'homme, 1973, pp. 97-106.

———. *Forme et signification: Essais sur les structures littéraires de Corneille à Claudel*. Paris: Corti, 1962.

Roy, Claude. «Le Roman d'analyse.» *La Nef*, 30 (1959), 61-66.

Russo, Paolo. «La Polemica sulla *Princesse de Clèves*.» *Belfagor*, 16 (1961), 555-602; 17 (1962), 271-98; 17 (1962), 385-404.

Rustin, J. «Notes sur les revendications de la sensibilité dans le roman du XVIIᵉ siècle.» *Travaux de Linguistique et de Littérature publiés par le Centre de Philologie et de Littérature Romanes de l'Université de Strasbourg*, 5.2 (1967), 35-47.

Saint-Réal, César Vichard de. *Don Carlos: nouvelle historique, 1672*. Ed. André Lebois. Avignon: Aubanel, 1964.

Sainte-Beuve, C.-A. «Madame de La Fayette.» *Critiques et portraits littéraires*. Paris: Bonnaire and Renduel, 1839, IV, 152-209.

Sarlet, Claudette. «La Description des personnages dans *La Princesse de Clèves*.» *XVIIᵉ Siècle*, 44 (1959), 186-200.

———. «Le Temps dans *La Princesse de Clèves*.» *Marche Romane*, 9 (1959), 51-58.

Sayce, R.A. *Style in French Prose: A Method of Analysis*. Oxford: Clarendon Press, 1953.

Scott, James W. «La Source d'un épisode de *La Princesse de Clèves*.» *Studi Francesi*, 33 (1967), 478-79.

Sebeok, Thomas A., ed. *Style in Language*. Cambridge: The MIT Press, 1960.

Segrais, Jean Regnauld de. *Oeuvres*. 2 vols. in 1. Nouvelle édition revue et corrigée. 1755; rpt. Geneva: Slatkine Reprints, 1968.

Senninger-Book, Claude-Marie. «*Le Bal du Comte d'Orgel*, une *Princesse de Clèves* du vingtième siècle.» *Symposium*, 17 (1963), 130-43.

Sfez, Fabien. «Le Roman polylexique du XVIIᵉ siècle.» *Littérature*, 13 (1974), 49-57.

Showalter, English, Jr. *The Evolution of the French Novel, 1641-1782*. Princeton: Princeton University Press, 1972.

Somaize, Antoine. *Le Dictionnaire des précieuses*. 2 vols. Paris: Jannet,

1856.

Sorel, Charles. *La Bibliothèque françoise*. Seconde édition revue et augmentée. Paris: Compagnie des libraires du Palais, 1667.

[Sorel, Charles] . *De la connaissance des bons livres ou Examen de plusieurs auteurs*. Amsterdam: Boom, 1673.

Sötér, István. *La Doctrine stylistique des rhétoriqueurs du XVIIᵉ siècle*. Budapest: Librairie Eggenberger Kossuth Lajos, 1937.

Spitzer, Leo. *Etudes de style*. Paris: Gallimard, 1970.

———. *Linguistics and Literary History: Essays in Stylistics*. New York: Russell and Russell, 1962.

Steiner, Arpad. «A French Poetics of the Novel in 1683.» *Romanic Review*, 30 (1939), 234-43.

Stendhal. «Walter Scott et 'La Princesse de Clèves.'» *Le National*, 48 (19 February 1830), 3-4.

Süpek, Otto. «La Dialectique du devoir et de l'amour dans *La Princesse de Clèves*.» *Acta Litteraria Academiae Scientiarum Hungaricae*, 15 (1973), 367-78.

Sweetser, Marie-Odile. «*La Princesse de Clèves* devant la critique contemporaine.» *Studi Francesi*, 18 (1974), 13-29.

———. «*La Princesse de Clèves* et son unité.» *PMLA*, 87 (1972), 483-91.

Taine, Hippolyte. «Mme de La Fayette—*La Princesse de Clèves*.» *Essais de critique et d'histoire*. 16th ed. Paris: Hachette, 1920, pp. 246-57.

Thibaudet, Albert. *Réflexions sur le roman*. Paris: Gallimard, 1938.

Tiefenbrun, Susan W. «Analytische Dialektik in der *Princesse de Clèves*.» *Poetica*, 5 (1972), 183-90.

———. «The Art of Repetition in *La Princesse de Clèves*.» *Modern Language Review*, 68 (1973), 40-50.

———. «A Structural Stylistic Analysis of *La Princesse de Clèves*.» Diss. Columbia, 1971.

Todorov, Tzvetan. «Les Catégories du récit littéraire.» *Communications*, 8 (1966), 125-51.

———. «La Description de la signification en littérature.» *Communications*, 4 (1964), 33-39.

———. «Les Etudes de style, bibliographie sélective.» *Poétique*, 1.2 (1970), 224-32.

———. *Littérature et signification*. Paris: Larousse, 1967.

———. *Poétique de la prose*. Paris: Seuil, 1971.

———, ed. *Théorie de la littérature*. Paris: Seuil, 1965.

Turnell, Martin. *The Novel in France*. London: Hamilton, 1950.

Ullman, Stephen. *Language and Style*. New York: Barnes and Noble, 1966.

———. *Style in the French Novel*. Oxford: Blackwell, 1964.

Valincour, Jean Baptiste. *Lettres à Madame la Marquise \*\*\* sur le sujet de la Princesse de Clèves*. Ed. Albert Cazes. Paris: Bossard, 1925.

Van Rutten, Pierre. «Style et signification dans *La Princesse de Clèves*.» *Le Français dans le Monde*, 36 (1968), 16-21.

Varga, Áron Kibédi. «La Désagrégation de l'idéal classique dans le roman de la première moitié du XVIII$^e$ siècle.» *Studies on Voltaire and the Eighteenth Century*, 26 (1963), 965-98.

———. «Pour une définition de la nouvelle à l'époque classique.» *CAIEF*, 18 (1966), 53-65.

Verschoor, Jan A. *Etude de grammaire historique et de style sur le style direct et les styles indirects en français*. Groningen: Druk, 1959.

Vier, Jacques. «La Princesse de Clèves.» *Littérature à l'emporte-pièce*. 5th series. Paris: Les Editions du Cèdre, 1969, pp. 22-42.

Vigée, Claude. *«La Princesse de Clèves* et la tradition du refus.» *Critique*, 159-60 (1960), 723-54.

Villedieu, Mme de [Marie-Catherine Desjardins]. *Les Désordres de l'amour*. Ed. Micheline Cuénin. Geneva: Droz, 1970.

Watt, Ian. *The Rise of the Novel: Studies in Defoe, Richardson and Fielding*. Berkeley and Los Angeles: University of California Press, 1964.

Weisz, Pierre. «L'Envers de la tragédie?» *Incarnations du roman: La réalité et les formes*. Saint-Aquilin-de-Pacy (Eure): Mallier, 1973, pp. 33-57.

———. «Tragédie et vérité romanesque: *La Princesse de Clèves*.» *Esprit créateur*, 13 (1973), 229-40.

Werman, Marjolyn R. «A Linking Image in *La Princesse de Clèves*.» *Romance Notes*, 13 (1971), 130-31.

Woshinsky, Barbara R. *«La Princesse de Clèves»: The Tension of Elegance*. Paris and The Hague: Mouton, 1973.

Yarrow, Philip J. *A Literary History of France*. Vol. 2 of *The Seventeenth Century (1600-1715)*. London: Benn, and New York: Barnes and Noble, 1967.

Zambon, Maria Rosa. *Bibliographie du roman français en Italie au XVIII$^e$ siècle: Traductions*. Florence: Sansoni Antiquariato, and Paris: Didier, 1962.

Zumthor, Paul. *Miroirs de l'amour: tragédie et préciosité*. Paris: Plon, 1952.

———. «Le Sens de l'amour et du mariage dans la conception classique de l'homme (Mme de la Fayette).» *Archiv für das Studium der neueren Sprachen und Literaturen*, 181, new series 81 (1942), 97-109.